The Clinic, Memory: New ~~~ ¹ ~

Elaine Feinstein read Engli.
for a quarter of a century wi
supervising undergraduates an
as well as reviews for London   ___ at
major festivals across the world   _ .ιanslated into most
European languages. In 1981 Feinstein was made a Fellow of the
Royal Society of Literature and later served on its Council. In 1990
she received a Cholmondeley Award for Poetry, and was given
an Honorary D.Litt from the University of Leicester. Her novel
Mother's Girl was shortlisted for the Los Angeles Times Fiction Prize
in the same year. Her first novel, *The Circle* (1970) was longlisted
for the 'lost' Man Booker prize in 2010. Her five biographies
include *Ted Hughes: The Life of a Poet* (2001; 2016), shortlisted for
the Marsh Biography Prize; and *Anna of all the Russias: The Life
of Anna Akhmatova* (2005), which has been translated into twelve
languages, including Russian. She has served as a judge for all the
major literary awards, and was Chair of the Judges for the T. S. Eliot
Prize in 1995. She received an Arts Council Award for her work on
The Russian Jerusalem (2004).

Also by Elaine Feinstein

POETRY
In a Green Eye · 1966
The Magic Apple Tree · 1971
At the Edge · 1972
The Celebrants and Other Poems · 1973
Some Unease and Angels · 1977
The Feast of Eurydice · 1980
Badlands · 1987
City Music · 1990
Daylight · 1997
Gold · 2000
Talking to the Dead · 2000
Cities · 2010
Portraits · 2015

FICTION
The Circle · 1970
The Amberstone Exit · 1972
The Glass Alembic · 1973
Children of the Rose · 1975
The Ecstasy of Dr Miriam Garner · 1976
The Shadow Master · 1978
The Survivors · 1982
The Border · 1984
Mother's Girl · 1988
All You Need · 1989
Loving Brecht · 1992
Dreamers · 1994
Lady Chatterley's Confession · 1995
Dark Inheritance · 2000
The Russian Jerusalem · 2008

TRANSLATION
Marina Tsvetaeva, *Bride of Ice: New Selected Poems* · 2009

AS EDITOR
After Pushkin · 1999

BIOGRAPHY
Ted Hughes: The Life of a Poet · resissued 2016

ELAINE FEINSTEIN

The Clinic, Memory
New and Selected Poems

CARCANET

First published in Great Britain in 2017 by
Carcanet Press Limited
Alliance House, 30 Cross Street,
Manchester, M2 7AQ
www.carcanet.co.uk

A CIP catalogue record for this book is available from the British Library.

ISBN 9781784103200

Typeset by XL Publishing Services, Exmouth
Printed and bound in England by SRP Ltd, Exeter

The publisher acknowledges financial assistance from Arts Council England

Supported by
ARTS COUNCIL
ENGLAND

Contents

From GOLD

From TALKING TO THE DEAD

From CITIES

From PORTRAITS

New Poems

Hair

How can I reassure my dismayed self in the mirror
     as a hank of hair comes away in the comb?
The stuff is soft and pale, as if from a days-old baby,
     and the shorn face looking back from the glass
reminds me of those bewildered French women
     with scalps exposed and features suddenly huge

whose heads were shaved for sleeping with German soldiers.
     My hair loss is only the common response
to chemicals which enter the blood searching out
     cancer cells that have escaped surgery.
Nothing hurts. I don't feel ill. I simply sit
     here, in my white pod, listening for beeps.

With what insensate vanity did I once give my age
     with such precision as the years went by
as if to invite astonishment? Dunbar had Pride
     lead in his 'Dance of the Seven Deadly Sins'
with wild demeanour – bonnet on one side –
     I must be one of her progeny.

Once I was a witch on a bicycle with two small boys
     late for school, holding on to me tightly,
my tangled hair trailing behind as I pedalled.
     Did I know I was happy then?
I was young at least, and commuting a hundred miles
     daily – though still behind with the mortgage.

And we loved the huge house we couldn't afford, the raspberry
     brambles and wild roses in the garden,
our library where my first poems took shape –
     the terracotta ceiling and sanded floor, where
young poets often came to sprawl and talk of their
     messy lives, and the erotic charge

of American poetry, or hearing Jeremy Prynne
　　　as he paced the floor, allowing us all to share
Aristeas' vision of nomadic tribes and their purity
　　　we all believed in – at least as he spoke of it.
Less innocent intoxications: London days,
　　　floating in wanton drift away from home,

listening at *Better Books* or drinking in pubs
　　　on Charing Cross Road with Andrew Crozier
– beautiful boy, and effortless lyric poet – the litter
　　　of whose lines aroused my own.
Long gone, those days. And now, my bushy hair.
　　　I go to buy a woolly hat against the cold

and a glamorous wig from Notting Hill. Once there,
　　　I stare through the glass window at shelves
of plaster dollies with tiny features, each face
　　　as splendidly null as Tennyson's Maud.
Even before entering I hate them all. I refuse
　　　to think beyond the months of treatment to come.

A curly white fur now covers my head. Some like it.
　　　I'm not sure, though I've junked the wig,
and today coming back from the hospital in sunshine
　　　through Regents Park, I watched
the branches of bare trees catch November gold
　　　and was suffused with extravagant happiness.

Mirror Talk

Is that my mother now behind the glass, looking
        dark-eyed and weary, as if doubting
whether I can be trusted to count pills,
        check blood sugar, or put lancets
into a sharps box? She is reproaching me,

a child too often lost in songs and stories. I know
        mine was to be the life she never lived,
the one she imagined as a gentle girl,
        a rich man's daughter in an office job,
with older brothers at university. She never dared

to flout her crabby father as her sister did.
        My father loved her smile,
she loved his working-class ebullience
        but they married late,
and I was their only child. Mother,

in middle age, you explained unhappily
        (I wanted a brother)
how Rhesus-negative blood made you miscarry,
        and later babies died and left you ill –
there could be no children after me.

I turned away from your shyness and delicacy –
        so slender-wristed, slim fingered,
all your shoes size three – not seeing the stamina
        you needed to live alongside
my father's euphoric generosity, his drama

of disaster and resilience or how his laughing
        indulgence stole my love
while you read school reports, met teachers, dabbed
        my chickenpox at night, feeling
it was always to him I turned in adoration.

When Cambridge against the odds welcomed me in,
    a Midlands Grammar School girl
with some talent but no self-discipline,
    always lacking worldly common sense
you mistook my precocity for ambition,

but I was only a wistful dreamer. A contender
    needs focus and direction.
I muddled on, loving the wrong men, until
    married and bearing a third child I heard
your sigh: 'I thought you were going to be so clever!'

I did not emulate my uncles' lives, spent graciously
    in serving public good,
their pleasure: clubs, fine meals, and cultured friends.
    Mother, forgive me, I did all I could.
They won position. I wrote poetry.

Delusions of the Retina

In winter I can invent a double-decker bus
    out of a red lorry and two lit windows

or walking in rain, see car headlights
    grow insectivorous feelers

tangled leads to the computer trick me
    into thinking I have found my reading glasses

but today spring touched the street magnolia
    into blossom, and now like a girl

with wet feet and muddy skirt I hurry
    to welcome another year into my garden.

Battleground

These Dunkirk victories of old age:
    another year, another
late spring. I'm back from hospital,

I've learned to walk without a stick
    feel safe in the shower, and open
the front door when I can't see the keyhole.

Crossing a road remains perilous
    but if I pause beside
a neglected garden, yellow roses

smell of Summer, and new leaves soften
    the poplars' stubby branches,
last year's pollarding forgotten.

So I rejoice in the seasons of the mortal
    even as I let myself imagine
this local war is one I am going to win.

Loving Don Quixote

Even now I love you, gentle Knight
    of the Rueful Countenance,
because I have always fallen most deeply
    in love with vulnerable men –
not losers exactly, but dream-led searchers,
    driven by a mad need to excel –
boldly pursuing glory in second-hand clothes
or – like my father, who left school at twelve –
    wearing his top hat in the President's box.
Yet they were nobler than the world they entered,
    their poor decisions readily now forgiven
as we forgive children who contrive
    to seek honour without calculation
simply to make sense of being alive.

The Impossible Rescue

My love, I dreamed of you again last night.
      We were exploring our old home
in Cambridge – Park Parade, I think –
      the details fade – but towards daybreak
you called my name out from another room
      calmly at first, then urgently
as if you were hurt and being brave:
      Hurry, Elaine, soon it will be too late!
I dragged myself out of sleep to respond
      but once awake
understood: there is no one now to save.

Betrayal

A response to Shakespeare's Sonnet 116

Get over it, get a life, my friends implored me,
     sure that revival lay in moving on.
Yet some bond held me like a tie of blood,
     as inescapable as the loyalty
formed in my father-adoring childhood.
     I could go anywhere now you were gone

but everywhere else was where I felt alone.
     Was that need for you – *love*?
There are harsher words. Cowardice is one,
     another, pride. I never could get rid of
my spoilt child's sullen grip on a possession –

I could not give up what once held us together:
     our bodies' casual tenderness –
our sleep's embrace become a natural tether.
     dispelling loneliness,
we both found home in a shared family nest
     and our licensed disorder.

Could I abandon that long happiness?
     Visits from old lovers easily
stirred sexual memories but I confess
     none of them could arouse me:
at best, they felt somehow irrelevant.
     I would not fake excitement,

I waited – though the rejected rarely win.
     Let's have no reassurance:
When you came back, of course I let you in –
     and yet it took endurance.
We were one flesh. So your guilt punished me
     and we both shared the pain of treachery.

Houdini's Last Trick

Driven to stunt after stunt:
    handcuffed in water,
buried underground

you would emerge triumphant.
    Cops double-locked their cells
but you broke out. Rivals

without your ingenuity
    never collected that ten
thousand dollars you laid down.

You shook off any claim
    to supernatural powers –
artifice was the game,

trained lungs, hard muscles,
    and an athlete's discipline
underpinned your puzzles.

Heroic: a dead Rabbi's son
    who poured gold coins
into a mother's apron.

Invited in to Royal palaces.
    With Conan Doyle – whose wife
wrote spirit messages –

you went to visit stylish mediums,
    and were dismayed
to see through all the mysteries displayed.

It became a crusade. At séances
    which banned your presence
you would use disguise. Or hired spies.

Newspapers ran your stories.
    One spirit guide
foretold your death – which you defied.

But did you wonder when you left
    a secret code word
with your wife, was it so absurd

to imagine, once outside the town glare
    of being alive,
that spirits become visible there

like stars on a clear night?
    And if anyone could break out
from an after-world, surely you might?

The thousands of fans at your funeral
    half-expected an escape, as if
for you death would never be final,

there had to be one last trick – almost afraid
    some lintel might suddenly crack
and a terrible window break open –

until that Wand of Rosewood was broken
    by the President of Magicians,
with due ceremony, over the coffin.

Cygnet

For a child bullied at her new school

Once I watched two swans glide over the Cam,
    silently powered by invisible feet,
their necks poised in a delicate curve as they swam:
    cool, white creatures in Summer heat.
At the waterside some ducks at noisy play
    were tipping upside down,
and fussing, as the royal birds went on their way.

In Ireland, I saw a group of swans rising
    from a millpond, with tough
muscled necks stretched out in a line,
    one wing-flap was enough
to take them upward with alarming power
    over a cluster of ducklings
scrabbling sociably in the mud together.

When I was told, my pretty girl, of cyber
    bullies on your mobile phone,
I remembered Hans Andersen's tale of ducklings
    harassing a cygnet on its own.
May his old fairy tale be set in bronze!
    Children mock the face of any stranger –
but some newcomers grow up into swans.

The Old Country

In Ukraine a woman who could be my ancestor
      boils forest roots. Old at forty-two,
she is shrivelled by winter. Her husband
      went to fight invaders
   and there is no news of him.
      Diphtheria and typhus ravage
what is left of the village.

In Western comfort I pity her harsh life.
      Yet angels walk beside her,
and her husband – no longer angry
      and redeemed from vodka –
is waiting for her on the far shore
      of that world we no longer believe in.

The News Channel

Shall we listen to the news?

In the little streets which smell of chocolate
round the Golden Square in Brussels
there are armed police

What news.   There is no news.

Once I inherited fear in the stories of
borders and slippery mud on river banks,
bribes and guards and angry dogs.

Now we watch on household screens
as fences of razor wire cross
quiet European fields.

When my grandfather spoke of Odessa
he remembered the music in street cafés,
acacia trees, and summertime on *Deribasovskaya.*

In tents across Europe now they remember Syria:
the ancient stones, the grand restaurants.

My grandfather did not want to serve
in the hated Tsar's army – these men too
are sick of a long war and carry children

but we are afraid of them
because they are numerous.

What news.   There is no news.

Old Days

In the smell of woodsmoke and dry leaves I remember:
    a glorious Cambridge of *copains*,
film-lit by Truffaut, Aznavour, Brassens,
    lifelong friendships long since over,
when I fell in love unsuitably with
    clever schoolboys or narrow-hipped dancers,
a Moroccan met on the boat from Marseilles,

and you, my partner in a long marriage,
    a man whose fingers were shy
and whose hug was clumsy, yet whose presence
    always gave me a sense of safety
for all your Walter Matthau grumpy wit.
    These days I am not much alone
yet I often think of you when I sing of life's gaiety.

Writing to Jane Eyre

After looking at Paula Rego's illustrations to Charlotte Brontë's novel

Here in the Portuguese version, Jane,
      you are wearing a black *ruched* dress –
puny – your hair severely combed –
      a fierce child, with a book of birds
and a wild need for love.
      No one so passionate is plain,

but without money – what else could you be
      but a governess?
The fairy tale takes you from Board School
      – brown dinge, hunger and porridge greys –
into the tranquil gardens of Thornfield Hall,
      where Mr Rochester's fall arouses tenderness.

His gibes and wheedling tricks soon tempt you
      to play his cruel game – more dangerous
than the terrors in the attic, more hurtful
      than the pain of jealousy –
until your scruples force you to abandon
      the chance of happiness.

Your stern refusal brings no peace.
      Only the mad woman's fire
destroying Thornfield Hall and
      his sightless cry reaching into you,
leave you free to embrace true servitude.
      Marry him, Jane! You will wear cerulean blue.

Ode to My Car

Farewell, my gallant friend! Loyal
        as an old dog, you've waited for me
outside so many doors, always responsive
        to the first turn of a key.
You were my freedom.   I could always leave.

You never failed me, not even in snow.
        On unknown winter roads
I could travel safe and warm,
        your solid frame enclosed me
like a parental hug, and I was soothed
        by the voice of your radio.

Now I am helpless, cannot run away.
        And standing at a windy bus stop
have to say: You were my good times,
        a piece of genuine, twenty-first-century magic –
my scratched old five-door Vauxhall automatic!

Last Muse

A bossy ghost I work for: she
      who only lives in words on the page
and has no thoughts I do not give her.

She has no flesh, and will not age.
      Why should I care
if she survives when I am gone?

And yet I do, though well advised
      most of us fall into the bag
of the forgotten or despised –

knowing if traces do remain
      they will not make us
live again – still carry on.

From

In a Green Eye

Father

The wood trade in his hands
at sixty-one back at the sawbench,
my stubborn father sands and planes
birchwood for kitchen chairs.

All my childhood he was a rich man
unguarded purchaser
of salmon trout, off-season strawberries
and spring in Switzerland.

Bully to prudish aunts
whose niggard habits taught them to assess
honest advantage, without rhetoric:
his belly laughter overbore their tutting.

Still boss of his own shop
he labours in the chippings without grudge
loading the heavy tables,
shabby and powerful as an old bus.

Calliope in the Labour Ward

she who has no love for women
married and housekeeping

now the bird notes begin
in the blood in the June morning
look how these ladies are
as little squeamish as
men in a great war

have come into their bodies
as their brain dwindles to
the silver circle on
eyelids under sun
and time opens

pain in the shallows to wave up and over them

grunting in gas and air
they sail to a
darkness without self
where no will reaches

in that abandon less
than human
give birth
bleak as a goddess

Mother Love

You eat me, your
nights eat me
Once you took
haemoglobin and bone
out of my blood

Now my head
sleeps forward on my neck
holding you

In the morning my
skin shines hot
and you are happy
banging your fat hands,

I kiss your
soft feet mindless:
delicately

your shit slides out
yellow and
smelling of curd cheese.

At Seven a Son

In cold weather on a
garden swing, his legs
in wellingtons rising over
the winter rose trees

he sits serenely
smiling like a Thai
his coat open, his gloves
sewn to the flapping sleeves

his thin knees working
with his arms
folded about the
metal struts

as he flies up
(his hair like long
black leaves) he
lies back freely

astonished in
sunshine as serious
as a stranger he is
a bird in his own thought.

Greenhouse

Blue stars and their
cold light of April 2 a.m.
watering these tomatoes:

Peaceful, plants are,
flowers for sex   no
moving out of their pots

green flesh   their
bruises leak a
liquid tart as smoke

and quietly our planet
fills with their
fibres

here under glass
they climb without eyes
like a rain forest

A Dream of Spinsterhood

'The wish for an unthinking reckless solitude' – Franz Kafka

All that Sunday
for a beginning deserts
of space
a bright self
moving single as a blade

or cruising
bodiless as a ghost
through London streets
an eye   invisible
in noise and light

But when last night
dreaming with a dry mouth
I was 25
again   alone
obsessed with sex

I cried out
caught in a
Sunday tight
as a box
and woke up weeping

to touch you in relief:
over us
leaves moved on the
ceiling gentle as
water on the roof
of a stone bridge.

Drunken Tuesday

Old nag I
hack on burning
with care with
hurrying stooped and
tugged at in
cold air 'money
money money'
eating at the
soft roes of the brain

Sourpuss, drag:
for what so partisan
why not put on
euphoria in a
yellow glass
so the eyes rising
like red leaves at a
windscreen give
up their witness

Run out in
rain in pools of
streetlights buzzing
with whisky, walking
at car lights
unafraid of
hoot and brake?

The black cars
wait for me when
I wake, I hear the
hiss of tyres and
the silence of
wet metal:
and the mind widens
to make out the
name of that
immunity had
seemed so gentle

Bodies

At home now   the first grey
in the hollows,   morning in
the grass,   in the brick
I hold you sleeping

and see last night
a bang the back door opens
holding your arm you
white say don't
be frightened smiling
your loving mouth
but white you are white

on a window a
window was it
into the flesh of your arm:
hung in the lab
in the hum of a
ship's hold, no one
to hear or help you

O you are stitched and
safe now, my fingers
feel you, I can
taste the oil in your
skin, your salty hair

knowing your blue
strings where the blood is
wanting you safe in
hard and shining steel
or tough as mineral, so
even a thin spirit of you
could be unkillable

Politics

Later the cleaners come
cigarettes pinched in their lips
as they lean gossiping

and they are gristle and bone
innocent elbows
scrubbing out urinals
with silent eyes dreaming

washing the cupboards
watching the time to be done

and the baize door is open
the torturers
are outside in the sun

Song of Power

For the baiting
children in my
son's school class who
say I am a witch:
black is the
mirror you give me

drawn inward at siege
sightless, mumbling:
criminal, to bear three
children like fruit
cannot be guarded
against enemies

Should I have lived sterile?
The word returns me.
If any supernatural power
my strangeness earns me
I now invoke, for
all Gods are

anarchic even the Jews'
outside his own laws, with
his old name
confirms me, and I
call out for the
strange ones with wild hair

all the earth over to
make their own coherence,
a fire their children
may learn to bear at last
and not burn in.

From
Poetry Introduction 1

Marriage

Is there ever a new beginning when every
word has its ten years weight, can there be
what you call conversation between us?
Relentless you are as you push me
to dance and I lurch away from you
weeping, and yet can we bear to lie
silent under the ice together like
fish in a long winter?

A letter now from York is a reminder of
windless Rievaulx, the hillside moving through
limestone arches, in the ear's liquid the
whirr of dove notes: we were a fellowship of three
strangers walking in northern brightness, our
searches peaceful, in our silence the
resonance of stones only, any celibate
could look for such retreat, for me
it was a luxury to be insisted on
in the sight of those grass overgrown dormitories.

We have taken our shape from the
damage we do one another, gently as
bodies moving together at night, we amend
our gestures, softly we hold our places:
in the alien school morning in the
small stones of your eyes I know how
you want to be rid of us, you were
never a family man, your virtue is
lost, even alikeness deceived us
love, our spirits sprawl together
and both at last are distorted

and yet we go toward birthdays and other
marks   not wryly   not thriftily
waiting, for where shall we find it, a
joyous, a various world? in fury
we share, which keeps us, without
resignation: tender whenever we touch   what
else we share   this flesh   we
bring together   it hurts to
think of dying as we lie close

From
The Magic Apple Tree

Anniversary

Suppose I took out a slender ketch from
under the spokes of Palace pier tonight to
catch a sea going fish for you

or dressed in antique goggles and wings and
flew down through sycamore leaves into the park

or luminescent through some planetary strike
put one delicate flamingo leg over the sill of your lab

Could I surprise you? or would you insist on
keeping a pattern to link every transfiguration?

Listen, I shall have to whisper it
into your heart directly: we are all
supernatural   every day
we rise new creatures   cannot be predicted

Out

The diesel stops. It is morning. Grey sky
is falling into the mud. At the waterside
two builders' cranes are sitting like birds

and the yellow gorse pushes up
like camel-thorn between oil-drums and old cars.
Who shall I take for my holy poet

to lead me out of this plain? I want an
innocent spirit of invention: a Buster Keaton
to sail unnaturally overhead by simple leverage and

fire the machinery. Then we should all spring out of our
heads, dazzled with hope, even the white-faced ticket
collector dozing over his fag, at such an intervention

suddenly in this stopped engine, we should
see the white gulls rising out of the rain over
the fen   and know our own freedom.

The Magic Apple Tree

Sealed in rainlight one
November sleepwalking afternoon streets
I remembered Samuel Palmer's garden
Waterhouse in Shoreham, and at once
I knew: that the chill of wet
brown streets was no more literal
than the yellow he laid there against
his unnatural blue   because
together they worked upon me like
an icon   infantine

he called his vision   so it was
with the early makers of icons, who
worked humbly, choosing wood without resin.
They stilled their spirits before using the gold
and while the brightness held under the *kvass*
their colours too induced
the peculiar joy of abandoning restlessness

and now in streets where only white
mac or car metal catches the failing
light, if we sing of
the red and the blue and the texture of goat hair,
there is no deceit in our prophecy:
for even now our brackish waters can
be sweetened by a strange tree.

Onion

Onion on the piano under the music
yesterday I found you
had put out fine
green curves of new life

hopelessly out of the earth
the park is
delirious with March snow
and my mission is to remove your
hiding place   and all places of hiding

so that nothing can come of you
though you consume yourself wholly:
you are tender and green, but
            I must put you into the bin.

Our Vegetable Love shall Grow

Shaking in white streetlight in
a cold night wind, two luminous blue fangs
push through the grass at the bus shelter:
an early crocus, drawing colour from
some hidden underfoot bulb. And now, mindless
desperate lonely waiting in a fen wind, we
barely move in our great coats, while that
blue piece of adventuring
takes all the electric of human light into
the beauty of its present flesh.

For The Beatles

Lived for 3 days on
coffee and bread, pinched
with the hope of getting clear
and over the radio again and
again shrewdly that electronic
track reached into me, yes
hoarsely their voices name it
the euphoric power, and the
badgered, even the mean and
the timid rise like
Japanese water flowers
in that spirit: old
impersonal rewardless easy
drum drum drum drum drum
Love is all you need

Bathroom

My legs shimmer like fish
my hair floats on the water:
tonight I observe that my
skin is no longer smooth
that blue veins show
in my arms that my
breasts are smaller

and lie seeing still water
meeting a white sky
(my elbows swim for me)
waiting for those
queer trails of thought
that move toward sleep

to where
the unforgiven words are
stored in circuits
of cells that hold
whatever shape there is
of the lost days

The Telephone, Failing Again

This public box is
the only light in the whole terrace:
a single bulb in the wet
hedge, with the wind rising.
And the harsh buzz in
my ear   carries me
over some border to where it seems
we could just
lose one another this way
like unpaired shoes in
some accident of disorder,
and I cannot even trust
you would notice the loss.
Where are you where
in what moon
house   do these dry
noises now release their dust?

Out of Touch

Now west down George Street a
star red as charred coal
blocks the line of the traffic

so that all the waiting cars
are made into shadows and
the street walls are red-stained

and into that March sun   you
move off lost   another shadow
against the stones of

a spectral city: love
don't be lonely   don't let us
always be leaving singly on

some bleak journey   wait for me:
this   deliberate world   is
rapidly losing its edge.

New Sadness / Old City

I saw Jerusalem from the Magog hills last night in
hot air the sky shaking:
white dust and crumbling stone and
the scent of scrubby hills

                              waterless
fort   Koheleth sadly and the
Egyptian before him whispers it
the death song of triumph   the desert
powders every man's eyelashes and
his cropped hair

                                    gentle city, will
the saints of the Lublin ghetto
enter your streets invisibly and
marvel at last   or fear to

as we listened like ghosts
in a parked car here breathless when
you were taken   tasting on
our teeth uneasily the strange
illicit salts of elation.

Renaissance Feb. 7

In the true weather of their art
these silver streets bustle, skin lit towers:
we have broken some magic barrier into
the daylight of the Duc de Berry's golden hours
and now in a supernatural city what is
possible changes as the
tones of tired voices lift
in the mild air
and like a tree
that might find loose birds in its
leafless hair, I am
open to the surprises of the season

From
The Celebrants

From *The Celebrants*

I

Remember Melusine
morose spectre, whose own superstition once
    made a serpent of her: she was
bewitched   into a myth   by chance
    out of her housekeeping because
she was credulous, and so wandered in
    bands of the spell-bound until
she fell into encephalitic trance. And still
    to her believing company she slithered
in green skin to the last day of her life.

II

Might be anyone's cracked daughter
sozzled, or skewed of vision, lonely,
in winter months invoking mutinous powers

that pour like mercury out of the moon
into the waiting mind with its own glass-lined
pumice craters and stains of orange oxide,

always the occult temptation, the erotic
world-flicker, shining in wet streets
like coal with streaks of mica, for

the demons rise at the first oblique
longing, they rise up nocturnal and cruel, and
the neophyte becomes their stammering mouth,

breaks into joy without drugs
dangerous, cannibal, frenetic with
forbidden knowledge, in deaf violence.

Bitten with toxic spiders, women
dance themselves into exhaustion knowing
the spirits that they bear are hostile

and yet are proud to be a hostage to them,
as if their hallucinations could be
a last weapon against humiliation:

Listen to their song: as
servants of the tribe they now
enter the crisis of their terror

willing to free us from the same service,
but their song draws us after them and
some will follow   into their own unreason.

III

Trees, under wet trees, I am beckoned down to a river
that runs into land through a sink of sedge and rushes,
white trench gas, between roots galled with witches fungus
cut stumps, where bodies of bald dogs stir at the crunch of my feet.

The mud and black leaves are frozen these last hours of the
year, I follow this sloping path downwards, like a lost sleeper, in
fear of finding the faces, and hearing the voices, of those
who came this way   by the black stub alder   and under

in frost against spindle shrubs, or wych elm in tangles of
twigs, and who swim in the smoke on the stream and beneath
the rotting bridge, and float head-high in the dark evergreen
yews, and hang waiting in that poisonous foliage.

Through hoots of long-eared owl, gunshot, and cries of
mallard across the marsh, what I fear is to hear their voices;
those obdurate spirits, haunted and harassed, who once
came down this route and laid waste their energies here

to become mares of god, crying, and singing epiphanies.
They offered their eyes and their entrails for the forest
spirits to fill them like swallow-tailed kites:
they bartered their lives and the air tastes of their drowning.

V

And this knowledge enters even
    between the bodies of lovers, though
we share each other's vigil: that our arms

hold water only, salt as the sea
    we come from, a spongework of
acid chains, our innermost landscape

an arcane pulp of flexible
    chemistry; sinus, tubes,
follicles, cells that wander

from red marrow in the crevices
    of our long bones across
membranes, blood-stream, thymus,

and lymph nodes   to defend
    our separate skin-bound
unit of internal territory.

Give me your astrolabe and now tell me
    what doing or refusing kills
or how we will our bodies treachery.

VIII

Fear the millennial cities
    jasper-lit, descending
with oil and wine and corn
    from ancient prophecies,

where men with lidless eyes
    through centuries will slither
in holy crystal streets
    on the blood of massacre.

Their secret flagellant rites
    and luminous scars declare
a godhead and release
    for any follower,

but every incarnation, from
    Schmidt of Thuringia, to
the lost of our Los Angeles
    reveals itself in murder.

And only the bitch leader
    of a Jenghis pack can show
a spite   as human as   adepts
    of those who call Messiah.

IX

Today the air is cold and bitter as kale
    the sky porcelain, the sun bleached
to white metal: I am alight with ions

awake   alert   under
    that ancient primal blue, which is
the serene accident of our atmosphere;

tethered by winter gold in
    the hair of these
bare willows on my own green waterside.

Here birds and poets may
    sing for their time
without intrusion from

either priest or physician;
	for the Lord relents; he is
faithful. In his silence.

Having no sound or name
	he cannot be conjured.
All his greatness is in this:

to free us from the
	black drama
of the magician.

Night Thoughts

Uncurtained, my long room floats on
	darkness, moored in rain,
my shelves of orange skillets
	lie out in the black grass.
Tonight I can already taste
	the wet soil of their ghosts.
And my spirit looks through the glass:
	I cannot hold on for ever.

No tenure, in garden trees, I
	hang like a leaf, and stare
at cartilaginous shapes
	my shadow their visitor.
And words cannot brazen it out.
	Nothing can hold for ever.

The Medium

My answer would have to be music
which is always deniable, since in my
silence, which you question, is only a landscape

of water, old trees and a few irresolute
birds. The weather is also inconstant.
Sometimes the light is golden, the leaves unseasonable.

And sometimes the ice is red, and the moon
hangs over it, peeled, like a chinese fruit.
I am sorry not to be more articulate.

When I try, the words turn ugly as rats and
disorder everything, I cannot be quiet,
I want so much to be quiet and loving

If only you wanted that. My sharpest thoughts
wait like assassins always in the dry wheat. They
chat and grin. Perhaps you should talk to them?

Nachtfest

Water black water at night the Rhine and
in small boats lanterns like
coloured souls solemnly passing

into darkness, into circles of silver, into
black quick currents of water hidden as
the trees that rise over us steeply

up to the pink stone of the Münster, floating in
floodlight, Erasmus lies there lost, the leaves of
green and gold tile are shining,

fountains of white fire pour down the living
cliffs of pine, over drinking Baselers, a
mist of flies

gathers around the bulbs of the
bandstand. Now on a darkened raft held by ropes invisibly
in the centre of the river

men prepare the festival rockets, when
in spasms of red and green those sticks shoot
into the sky, their

light draws our breath upwards, we are gone
over the low moon after them into a
black imagination of depth more final than water.

'The only good life is lived without miracles.'

(N. Mandelstam)

Under hot white skies, if we could,
in this city of bridges and pink stone live gratefully
here is a lacework of wooden ghosts from New Guinea
Etruscan jewels, beetles with scales of blue mineral.

Bad news follows us, however. I wonder if
anyone walks sanely in middle age. Isn't there
always some desperation for the taste of one last
miraculous fruit, that has to be pulled from the air?

From

Some Unease and Angels

Patience

In water nothing is mean. The fugitive
enters the river, she is washed free;
her thoughts unravel like weeds of
green silk: she moves downstream
as easily as any cold-water creature

can swim between furred stones, brown
fronds, boots and tins the river holds equally.
The trees hiss overhead. She feels their shadows.
She imagines herself clean as a fish,
evasive, solitary, dumb. Her prayer:
to make peace with her own monstrous nature.

By the Cam

Tonight I think this landscape could
    easily swallow me: I'm smothering
in marshland, wet leaves, brown
    creepers, puddled in
rain and mud, one little gulp and

I'll be gone without a splutter
    into night, flood, November, rot and
river-scud. Scoopwheeled for drainage.
    And by winter, the fen will be brittle and
pure again, with an odd, tough, red leaf frozen
    out of its year into the ice of the gutter.

Dad

Your old hat hurts me, and those black
    fat raisins you liked to press into
my palm from your soft heavy hand:
    I see you staggering back up the path
with sacks of potatoes from some local farm,
    fresh eggs, flowers. Every day I grieve

for your great heart broken and you gone.
    You loved to watch the trees. This year
you did not see their Spring.
    The sky was freezing over the fen
as on that somewhere secretly appointed day
    you beached: cold, white-faced, shivering.

What happened, old bull, my loyal
    hoarse-voiced warrior? The hammer
blow that stopped you in your track
    and brought you to a hospital monitor
could not destroy your courage
    to the end you were
uncowed and unconcerned with pleasing anyone.

I think of you now as once again safely
    at my mother's side, the earth as
chosen as a bed, and feel most sorrow for
    all that was gentle in
my childhood buried there
    already forfeit, now forever lost.

Coastline

This is the landscape of the Cambrian age:
   shale, blue quartz, planes of slate streaked with
iron and lead; soapstone, spars of calcite;
   in these pools, fish are the colour of sand,
velvet crabs like weeds, prawns transparent as water.

This shore was here before man. Every tide
   the sea returns, and floats the bladderwrack.
The flower animals swell and close over creatures
   rolled-in, nerveless, sea-food, fixed and forgotten.

My two thin boys balance on Elvan Stone
   bent-backed, intent, crouched with their string and pins,
their wet feet white, lips salt, and skin wind-brown,
   watching with curiosity and compassion:
further out, Time and Chance are waiting to happen.

From
Badlands

A Letter from La Jolla

On a balcony in California
being surprised by February
which is the sweet season here, when
blue-scaled grunion dance
on their tails, at high tide
on La Jolla sands, to mate there
and are caught in pails and eaten,

I write across distance and so much time
to ask, my one-time love, what happened to you?
Since my last letter which I meant to be
cruel as my own hurt could barb it, now
under yellow skies, pale sun, I sit
sucking fresh limes and thinking over
my childish spite, and how much life I've wasted.

I'm jealous of the sensible girl
you must have married long since.
Well, I've been happy, too.
Sometimes. You always knew
the shape I'd choose would never
be single or sober, and you did not need
what you once most admired.

Unswerving as you were, I guess
you must be prosperous, your children neat,
less beautifully unruly than my own
perhaps less talented, less generous;
and you won't know my work or my new name,
nor ever read my books.
Our worlds don't meet.

And yet I doubt if you have altogether
forgotten the unsuitable dark girl
you held all weekend in your parents' flat,
talking and talking, so this letter
comes to you this morning almost in play:
our thoughts once moved so easily together
like dolphins offshore to the land mass of the day.

The Water Magician of San Diego

for Joel

A blue pool wobbles in the sun.
Above me, like ocean weeds,
the strands of palm leaves flicker;
sticky ferns unroll their fronds;
the red helicopters hum,
like summer birds overhead;
and a local voice inquires:
How are you doing today?
What can I possibly say.

I'm trying to recover, but
I haven't quite learnt the smile.
And it may take quite a while
to look out over this ocean
that covers most of the planet
and not feel mainly alone.
My neighbour in the deckchair
is a Californian male.
And he senses a foreign spirit.

My books and scribble betray it.
So far he's not alarmed.
His handsome face is dimpled.
His hair cut short as fur;
and he has no fear of failure.
Don't wish him any harm,
but I'd like to see him waver.
– Hatfield, I murmur, Hatfield.
– Don't think I follow that.

– Don't you remember him?
He doesn't, and he finds my words
both dubious and grim.
– These, I say, are the Badlands,
won back from the dry brush and buzzard
for the entrepreneur and the bandit
these old hills, (the gold hills) favour.
Nowadays the realtors
take breakfast at La Valencia.

He doesn't understand. But
my eyes are deep and burning.
My face is aquiline.
I bring a whiff of danger;
Something is out of hand.
Perhaps I've fallen into
need (or even worse) bad luck,
which are sinister contagions
nobody here laughs off.

– Shall I confess the facts?
I've lived for five years now
as love's hypochondriac, and
it's hard to break the habit.
Is that what you're picking up?
Do you guess I've carried here
some intractable history?
(I'm teasing, but his face betrays
he's sorry now he woke me.)

– Hatfield the rainmaker?
He asks uneasily.
– The same, I nod, folk hero.
A native of your city.
A farm near San Diego
housed his earliest chemistry.
I thought you'd know his name.
Once City Halls in every County
echoed to his fame.

You needed him for water
on which this coast depends.
This strip may look like Paradise
but garden life could end.
Nothing here is natural.
The ice-plant spreads magenta
but these trees aren't indigenous.
Your water's brought from Boulder
and sprinklers cool the citrus.

Which is why you need magicians
(He's looking rather pale).
You will remember Hamelin?
No. Europe is far away.
The burghers learnt a lesson there.
Magicians must be paid.
Comfort and complacency
bring in their own revenge
– The whole thing's superstition!

– No doubt, I nod to this,
And yet his contracts were fulfilled.
The clouds formed as he promised,
the reservoirs were filled.
He was modest in his offer
to those areas parched for rain;
set evaporating tanks about,
his only claim, within a month,
Nature would end the drought.

He came when men were waiting.
Made an educated bet.
The councillors who hired him
must have known as much, and yet
they paid their fifty dollars out
with unconcealed relief.
The snag in San Diego
was the absence of belief.

Newspapers counted down the days
and gloated as they passed.
For being taken in, they mocked
the Mayor and all his staff.
(The charlatan's forgiven here
but no one trusts a victim.)
Lawyers sent to Hatfield
made manoeuvres which he met

with sardonic understanding,
and at once planned his departure.
The careful and the sober
should treat with great respect
whoever lives upon his wits.
Con-men, poker-players, poets
put the solid world at risk
and then enjoy the dance;
what happened then was in excess
of meteorological variance.

Rain? More than sixteen inches.
Flooded freeways, and carried off bridges.
There were bungalows dragged off their moorings.
And houses perched up on the cliff edge.
There was furniture floating on drainage.
There were hailstones like hens' eggs, and flashes
that carved out a creek through the desert.
Then mass panic.
Evacuation.

Abandoning motorised transport,
in rowboats, on surf boards and planks
the rich mostly got away early
but they couldn't call in at the banks.
My neighbour said with conviction:
– They'd have lynched him!
But I shook my head: It seems
Hatfield's contracts continued.
And the law wasn't ever called in.

My neighbour can't lie in his deckchair.
Perhaps he should take a quick swim?
Or calm his nerves in the Jacuzzi.
I feel almost friendly to him.
– Three wives, I should guess, lie behind you.
You're rich and you're healthy, and free.
Don't be anxious
or look for an answer
to some threat you imagine in me.

If I ever succeed in escaping
from this future where I am a stranger
and find myself back home in Europe
with those I most love out of danger;
as I fly back on some scheduled airline
(putting all my old pennies together)
when my spirit revives, I may well be
peppery, bold and alert there.
But I won't interfere with the weather.

England

Forgotten, shabby and long time abandoned
    in stubbled fur, with broken
teeth like toggles, the old gods are leaving.
    They will no longer crack the
tarmac of the language, open generous
    rivers, heal our scoured thoughts.
They will only blink, and move on, and
    tomorrow no one will remember their songs

unless they rise in warning, as when
    sudden planes speed overhead
crossing the sky with harsh accelerating
    screams. You may shiver then
to hear the music of the gods leaving.
    This generation
is waiting for the boy Octavius.
    They don't like losers.
And the gods are leaving us.

Park Parade, Cambridge

i.m. Elizabeth Bishop

Your thoughts in later years must, sometimes,
have visited this one-time lodging house,
the wood then chocolate brown, the plaster
veined, this bedroom floating over
spongy grass down to a shallow river.

As a mild ghost, then, look with me tonight
under this slant roof out to where
the great oak lies, its foliage disguised
with flakes of light. Above us, clouds
in these wide skies remain as still as sandbars.

Sleeplessly, together, we can listen
to the quiet song of water, hidden
at the lock, and wait up for the first
hiss of cycle tyres and whistling builders.
Fellow asthmatics, we won't even cough

because for once my lungs are clean,
and you no longer need to fight for breath.
And though it is by chance now I inherit
this room, I shall draw both tenderness and strength
from the friendly toughness of your spirit.

Hamburg

for Martin

You gave me all the riches of the city;
opera, pool-halls, all-night
Café Stern, cold Pils, and laughter;
the taste of coffee
with the first newspapers

and Isestrasse, over the canal,
street market stalls piled up
with edible truffles, beans
of black locust, poppy-seed buns,
and living fish.

We watched three carp swim there
in a glass tank; and knew
the bite of each grim
Asian jaw was meant to crush no more
than muddy weeds against a horny palate,

fierce yet vegetarian.
When the strongest fish leapt out
slap at our feet, it was your hand
that checked my squeamish terror.
My bold son,

learning to live without protection now
other than grace and beauty,
how I bless your spirit, as I
call up voice and face
to give me courage in this lonely place.

New Songs for Dido and Aeneas

I

The day opens, bland
and milky-blue. A woman
is looking out at a rain-washed garden.
In her thought a wooden flute and
spice trees, and the sun
flashing off the bracelet at her wrist.
She is no longer waiting for something to happen.

Her quiet face observes
the evidence of an order
older than Greece, in whose protection
the courtyard holds the trees, and
all her memories stir as gently
as leaves that flicker on the wall below her:
A stranger already knocks at the gate of the palace.

2

After Europe, Dido, all winter
the days rushed through me
as if I were dead, the
brown sea pouring into the cities
at night, the rain-smell of fish,

and when you ask for my story, how
we came to be blown along your
dock-streets, pocked and scuffed,
I see only my mother laced in silk,
myopic, her small feet picking over rubble.

How to make you imagine
our squares and streets, the glass
like falls of water, the gold-leaf
in the opera houses. There were
summer birds golden as weeds,

the scent of coffee and halva
rising from marble tables,
and on dark afternoons
the trams grinding on wet rails
round the corners of plaster palaces

such a babble of Empire
now extinguished, we can
never go home, Dido,
only ghosts remain
to know that we exist.

Some pain has burnt a desert in your head,
    which spills into the room,
sexless and stony-eyed, you rock
    over the landscape of your sandy dead.

I cannot soothe or reach into your dream
    or recognise the ghosts you name, or even
nurse your shaken body into calm.
    You wake, exhausted: to meet daylight in hell,

as the damned wake up with pennies
    of departure, and the ash
of all their lives have left undone
    lying like talcum on the tongue.

4

Unrepentant, treacherous, lecherous
    we loved beauty, in the tenderness
of violins, or the gentle voice of a girl,
    but we built over the stink of our dead,
our rivers ran yellow with the forgotten.
    Dido, the cruel cannot be blessed.

This endless sunshine, frangipani, gulls calling:
    How can you ease my pain or give me rest?
Ours was the generation that opened the gates
    to all the filthy creatures that had waited
for centuries to lay our cities waste.
    Your village kingdom cannot heal me now.
In any case, the cruel cannot be blessed.

Things come too late to save.
    On the last boat, we sang
old prayers, and some dreamed of quiet,
    but the sea took most of us. And
I am not prepared for white soot, cold ash,
    or the red sands of Australia. Forget me,
Dido. The cruel cannot be blessed.

Back from the seashore
  plangent, uncertain;
speaking of duties,
  but weaker, frightened.

The monster you found
  so gentle a beauty, is
no stranger here to us.
  You call her Venus;

but she is a mollusc
  goddess, pink in orifice,
prey clamped sweetly
  deep inside her ocean flesh.

What good mother would
  throw you to the ruthless seas?
Only the harshest
  and meanest of the deities.

You speak of yellow afternoons,
  dark skies, wet streets. And I who
once let the whole building of my own
  kingdom stop, to care for you,

offer my counsel; since
  it is in my gift
to curse or bless: be prudent, for
  you put us both in peril.

6

Last night, my sad Creusa crept
  quietly into my dream. As if
dry leaves could speak, she whispered,
  but I could not catch her words,
Dido, and I was afraid

of what had wakened her.
    She was a loyal wife, in times
when nothing was forbidden
    no pleasure thought too gross:
and contrition as poor-spirited as cowardice.

Shall I spread that disease
    over the known world in a single colour?
Dido, I swear that Venus' weather in the cave
    the day our mouths first opened to each other,
and sweetness ran in our veins, was innocent.

Monsters and blood I dream of now.
    and a long voyage, lost,
although the wind has filled our sails.
    I must not falter in my mission,
Dido, at whatever cost.

                    7

    Now in your leaving I admit old age.
    How else? a clutch of whiteness at the heart
    dry lips and icy wrists, a scream
    that cuts my face into a wooden gape

    At night   awake   alone   alert
    to cries of meat-eating birds,
    the whinge of gristle on bone, I sit
    propped up on pillows, choking

    on the catarrh of tears.
    Sick   and yet stubborn
    I, who was once your nurse,
    hold back the power of my ancient curse.

Now we leave harbour, I no longer
fear the years' exile
nor what serenity I've lost:
I shall be no footnote now or gloss.
Empire is mine.

New heirs will rise to impose their will
on strange planets that all still
remain unknown, and thus fulfil
my deepest lust.

In this I trust.

The pyre of pine
    and ilex is prepared
and moonlit herbs
    isn't that the tale
of Dido's final stroke
    to wet Aeneas' eyes
as smoke?

European lies:
    I come of harsher blood
long ago, the venom of
    scorpions ceased to harm
and I've learnt from
    cactus and desert grass
what to do without.

I recognise in you that
    juniper tree, top-heavy
with branches, who may be
    will try to seed
again in parched earth
    and salt land;
but will not stand.

While my own root
    goes deep, into soil where
mysterious waters keep their
    sources cool, and though my leaves
dry out, and the wild sands blow,
    I shall live my time.

And when my bones lie
    between white stones at last
and fine white dust
    rises over all, no one who
survives among the dead
    will scorn my ghost.

From *Two Songs from Ithaca*

I

My man is lost.
And yet his wisdom sings in my
innermost source of blood,
my flesh recalls his love.
We were one earth.

I hold the pain,
as I wait every day
to question sailors at the port,
and so endure their sly reports
of his delay.

No more than water
once to his moods,
even now though he lies
on a foreign coast,
I am drawn and pure;

and on his return
I shall bless the sea
and forgive whoever holds him
far away from me.
If he only lives.

3

Who brings a message over
the threshold of my dream? It is
Hermes, the twister, the pivoter, to remind me
of strangers, returning, who speak in the language
of timberwolves, feeding on human flesh, sorcerer's prey.
And I blench at his voice.

But I straighten awake.
Even if he is sick, huddled up,
with a grey face and seamed, my old love,
looking fierce or mad, my
Odysseus, bitter or black, I am his,
as I held back my own death for this:
so now I rejoice.

From *Songs of Eurydice*

I

The dead are strong.
That winter as you wandered,
    the cold continued, still
the brightness cut
    my shape into the snow:
I would have let you go.

Your mother blew
my dust into your lips
    a powder white as cocaine,
my name, runs to your nerves
    and now I move again in your song.
You will not let me go.

The dead are strong.
Although in darkness I was lost
    and had forgotten all pain
long ago: in your song
    my lit face remains
and so we go

over pools that crack
like glass, through forests shining
   black with twigs that wait
for you to wake them, I return
   in your praise, as Eurydice's
ghost I light the trees.

   The dead are strong.

                    2

River, green river, forget
   your worm-eaten gods,
for we come to sweeten you,
   feel how the air has grown
warm and wet now
   the winds have all fallen.

On bent willow boughs
   beads of yellow break open
winter creatures we roused
   giant beeches and scrubland
in white roots respond
   Orpheus   Orpheus

We release all the woodlands
   from sleep, and the predator birds
from their hungering,
   wild cats are calm
as we pass

   as we reach the fields
men with grey knuckles
   lean over furrows
and blink.
   In the villages

wives honed too thin
    with their riverside washing
now straighten up,
    listen and nod.
What are they remembering?

    In cities, the traders
leave market stalls; even
    the rich leave their
food tureens. No one
    collects or cleans
their dirty crockery.

    Click! All transistors off.
Traffic stops. In
    a voice, everyone
hears how much
    any soul touched
by such magic is human.

3

A path of cinders, I remember
    and limping upward
not yet uprooted from
    my dream, a ghost

with matted eyes, air-sacs
    rasping, white
brain, I staggered
    after you

Orpheus, when you first
    called, I pushed
the sweet earth from my mouth
    and sucked in

all the powders of volcanic ash
   to follow you
obedient up
   the crumbling slope

to the very last ridge –
   where I saw clumps of
yellow camomile in the dunes
   and heard the applause

of your wild mother
   great Calliope
crying good, my son, good
   in the fumes of the crater.

When the wiring sputtered
   at my wedding feast
she was hectic, glittering;
   her Arabian glass

burst into darkness
   and her flesh shimmered.
She was still laughing, there,
   on that pumice edge

with all Apollo's day behind her
   as I saw your heavy
shoulders turn. Your lips move.
   Then your eyes.

and I lay choking   Orpheus
   what hurt most then was
your stunned face
   lost

cruel   never to be touched
   again, and watching
a blown leaf in your
   murderous eye

shrivel …

5

Over many centuries
modest ladies
who long for splendour
                    gather here

their eyes most tender
their voices low
and their skins still clear
                    when they appear

and to Dionysus
they offer their bodies
                    for what they seek

The god of abandon
destroys their reason
                    Beware the meek!

6

You belonged to Apollo
    the gold one the cold one
and you were his servant:
    he could not protect you.

You called for your mother
    and her holy sisters
she wept as a witness:
    but could not protect you.

Here they come, murderers,
    their bodies spattered
with blood as they stagger
    off-balance towards you.

They claw and maul you
    with hoes and long mattocks
their heavy rakes tear at your
    throat and your fingers.

They batter the listening
    birds, and the oxen
at plough, and they share out
    the limbs of each creature they kill.

Any my love's head is thrown
    on the waters, it floats
singing still. All the
    nine Muses mourn,

Orpheus   Orpheus –
    for how many poets
must die at the hands
    of such revellers?

7

And the curse of all future
    poets to die by
rope or stake or fire falls there
    on these mindless creatures

no longer human their toes
    grow roots and their knees are
gnarled – their arms branch leaves:
    who will release them?

Their flesh is wood.

8

As dreamers now together
we forget Apollo's day
    that cruel light in which at last
all men become shadows;
    and we forgive even those
dead gods, who sleep among us.
    For all their gifts, not one
of them has power to summon us.
    In this green silence
we conceal our one true marriage.

From
City Music

Urban Lyric

The gaunt lady of the service wash
stands on the threshold and blinks in the sunlight.

Her face is yellow in its frizz of hair
and yet she smiles as if she were fortunate.

She listens to the hum of cars passing
as if she were on a country lane in summer,

or as if the tall trees edging this
busy street scattered blessings on her.

Last month they cut a cancer out of her throat.
This morning she tastes sunshine in the dusty air.

And she is made alert to the day's beauty,
as if her terror had wakened poetry.

Annus Mirabilis 1989

Ten years ago, beneath the Hotel Astoria,
    we watched a dissident cabaret in Budapest,
where they showed Einstein as a Jewish tailor.
    All the women on stage were elegantly dressed.

Their silken garments were cleverly slit to expose
    illicit glimpses of delicate thighs and breast.
Einstein was covered with chalk, in ill-fitting clothes;
    he was taking measurements, trying to please the rest.

At the climax of the play, to applause and laughter
     they raked him with strobe lights and the noise of guns.
I was chilled by the audience euphoria.
     Of course, I don't have a word of Hungarian,

and afterwards there were embarrassed explanations,
     which left out tailoring and obsequious gestures.
Their indignation was all about nuclear science, while
     I pondered the resilience of an old monster.

Hay Fever

When Timothy grass and Rye pollen flew
each year, I began to honk like a goose.

It was always summer and party time
for kissing and rolling in the grass

so I couldn't bear to stay at home in bed.
I painted my face with beige pancake

put drops in my eyes, and learnt instead
as my membranes flared and I gasped for air

how to feel out of things
even when there.

Valentine for a Middle-aged Spouse

Dear Love, since we might both be dead by now
through war, disease, hijack or accident
at least for one day let's not speak of how
much we have bickered, botched and badly spent.
Wouldn't it make much more sense to collude
in an affectionate work of camouflage,
turning our eyes away from all we've skewed
to the small gains of household bricolage?
As our teeth loosen and our faces crag
(I shall grow skinnier as you grow paunched,
a Laurel to your Hardy, not much brag),
I'll think of all our love most sweetly launched
if you will look with favour on these lines
we may still live as tender valentines.

Homecoming

The light is sullen today, yet people are
bustling in the rainy street under my window,

poking in the Cypriot grocers for aubergines,
buying their strings of garlic and onions;

they can choose between the many seeds on
the bread: rye, sesame, cumin.

Across the road, the pharmacy windows
are lettered in brass like a Victorian shop.

In the coffee house with its heavy green and gold
pottery, they serve bean soup with sausages

and the accents of old Vienna mingle
with California. In the countryside

every one of us would be found peculiar.
We'd leak away. In Englands Lane

(through road for taxis and the Camden hoppa)
this city music and a few friends keep me sane.

Getting Older

The first surprise: I like it.
Whatever happens now, some things
that used to terrify have not:

I didn't die young, for instance. Or lose
my only love. My three children
never had to run away from anyone.

Don't tell me this gratitude is complacent.
We all approach the edge of the same blackness
which for me is silent.

Knowing as much sharpens
my delight in January freesia,
hot coffee, winter sunlight. So we say

as we lie close on some gentle occasion:
every day won from such
darkness is a celebration.

From
Daylight

Homesickness

i.m. Maria Fadeyeva Enzensberger

Yesterday I found a postcard with your scrawl:
'Darling, we are all horses, how is it
you haven't learned that yet?' And at once
your high-boned, white face rose
beside me like a reproach

as if I had begun to forget the wildness
in the gutturals of your laugh, and
the loneliness of *toska po rodine*
in the frozen sea of your eyes. But I have not.
You were always my Russia:

the voice of Marina's poetry. We saw you last
in a Moscow of brown streets, puddles, and
people queuing for ice cream: an autumn of anomalies,
women turning back tanks – and in St Petersburg
there were teenage boys playing *Deutschland über alles*.

Your mother, the poet Aliger, brought us into
Sologub's yellow mansion where Ivan found himself
in his underpants and writers fix their *dachas*:
Bulgakov would have enjoyed the chicken livers in coriander.
That day you were shaking with the euphoria

of street victory, as if you had come home
after the bleakness that took you into
Highgate hospital. 'I have been so frightened,'
you whispered to me there and I had no answer,
any more than at your table in the Cambridge fens

rich with forest mushrooms, peppers and white cheese,
when you struck the glass to command some speech
of love and closeness, and we all failed you. In London
you found another silence, and now we're only left with
a little honey and sun from Mandelstam's dead bees.

Tony

It was February in Provence and the local market
sold goats' cheese wrapped in chestnut leaves and
thick, painted pottery. The stalls of dark check shirts
were the kind you used to wear, and we began to see you:
burly, bearded, handsome as Holbein's Wyatt,
looking into the eyes of a girl or
jumping up from the brasserie table
to buy truffles from a street vendor.

We stayed with our children like gypsies in a barn
of your wife's family house near Aix, and you fed us
beef *daube*, thrush pâté and wine. Long ago
we sat through the night as a threesome writing
those film reviews I always drove to Heffers
in the early rainlight of a Cambridge morning. We still own
the pearwood Dolmetsch bought at your urging,
and copies of that magazine you and I ran together

which the police came to investigate after
a delivery of *Naked Lunch* from Olympia.
For a few years, you moved whenever we did,
from Adams Road to Sherlock, then De Freville
where the printer we owed money lived next door.
You wrote your first book for three hours a day
and then felt restless, since your body liked
to use its energies and you could lift a car.

Your hair was thick and brown
even in York District Hospital where you murmured
'I'm not dying, am I?' and described
the wild animals calmed with a click in your throat.
We guessed you could withstand a February *mistral*
that gets under the clothes so bitterly down here
more easily than we can, being younger
and more robust though, strangely, no longer alive.

Insomnia

The moon woke me, the pocked and chalky moon
that floods the garden with its silvery blue

and cuts the shadow of one leafy branch across
this bed of ours as if on to bright snow.

The sky is empty. Street lights and stars
are all extinguished. Still the moon flows in,

drowning old landmarks in a magic lake,
the chilly waters lapping at my pillow,

their spell relentless as this cold
unhappiness in which I lie awake.

Eclipse

On both sides of the gardens the tall
houses have put out their lights.
Now the cypress is blue and furry,
night creatures move quietly in the long grass,
and, as if in the ages before electricity,

the moon is a white lantern over the birch trees.
Grandchildren, indulged after the Passover seder,
have stopped using the mouse on my apple mac
to stare through the window at the luminous ball
like primitive people in a world of miracles.

This year, Katriona read the questions from the Haggadah;
Lara knew the ancient stories. Now three generations
sit together, imagining ourselves on the globe
of the earth, and trying to believe it is our own
brown shadow moving over the moon.

Izzy's Daughter

'You must be Izzy's daughter,' they said.
I was a liquid, black stare. An olive face.

'So thin. Doesn't she eat? She reads too much.'
My teasing, brawny aunts upset my mother.

I wanted to be as reckless as my father,
to dive through rough, grey waves on Southport sands,

and shake the salt out of my hair as he did.
Instead, I shivered, blue with cold, on the shore.

But I was Maggie Tulliver, proud of my cleverness,
when the whole family listened to my stories.

He listened, too; troubled, his lips moving,
and dog-brown eyes following every word.

'Where does it all come from?' they marvelled at me.
My timid mother smiled from her quiet corner.

Bonds

There are owls in the garden and a dog barking.
After so many fevers and such loss,
I am holding you in my arms tonight, as if
your whole story were happening at once:
the eager child in lonely evacuation
waking into intelligence and then
manhood when we were first *copains*,
setting up tent in a rainy Cornish field, or
hitchhiking down to Marseilles together.

You were braver than I was and so
at your side I was never afraid, looking for
Dom 99 in the snows of suburban Moscow,
or carrying letters through Hungarian customs,
I learnt to trust your intuitions more than my own,
because you could meet Nobel laureates,
tramps and smugglers with the same confidence,
and your hunches worked, those molecular puzzles,
that filled the house with clay and wire models.

In the bad times, when like poor Tom Bowling,
you felt yourself gone for ever more,
and threw away all you deserved, you asked me
What was it all for? And I had no answer, then
or a long time after that madness;
nor can I now suggest new happiness,
or hope of good fortune, other than
staying alive. But I know that lying at your side
I could enter the dark bed of silence like a bride.

Fyodor: Three Lyrics

I

In Bad Homburg, I watched him over the tables,
the homely face, false teeth, poor clothes.
I'm a Swiss doctor, but I read novels.

When he had lost every coin from his worn purse
he looked up at me and smiled:
'I am a man,' he said, 'without a future.'

I had treated him the night before
for epilepsy, and he spoke then of
the joy he felt while lying on the floor

one moment before the foam and spasms.
His face was shining there as he explained:
'Christ alone,' he said, 'can save Russia.'

2

In Basel, the church floats in the moon
and the trees whiten. There is no casino.
I met him once again with his new wife,

looking at Holbein's coffined Christ,
that decomposing body, green and blue,
the swollen limbs like ripened gooseberries.

He turned, and though he did not recognise
my face, answered my greeting so:
'I shall burn everything I once worshipped.'

3

What were his sins, then, more than recklessness,
disorder, and a young wife's jewels pawned?
I sometimes wonder if perhaps his genius

(so foreign to this sober, cobbled city
piled above gorges where the black Rhine flows)
had in the very sob of its own pity

another throb of cruelty and pleasure
that made the writing shimmer. Well, I know
I do more human good here as a doctor.

Wigmore Hall

for Martin

In July heat, beneath the frieze of blue where
golden Apollo stands beneath muse and scribe,
the four musicians have removed their jackets;
and in red braces, silver flute in hand,
you pause to smile, and wipe your misted glasses.

Long ago, when you were at school in
Grantchester Meadows, one speech day
in a hot school hall, your hair too long,
untidy, you came on at eight years old,
after the madrigals to play a folk song,

and the sleepy audience of bored
parents and fellow pupils waiting for
the distribution of prizes, slowly began to attend
and burst into applause when the song ended.
You were surprised, and a shy smile

transformed your face. Let's hope
tonight there's no Apollo to be envious
of these notes singing out in curving line,
as you risk putting yourself to the test
rather than dream 'I might have been' from a desk.

Staking Tomatoes

for Adam

The leaves of four droopy tomato plants
release tobacco harshness, as your fingers
that know their way through Chopin on the piano,
try clumsily to tie these stems to a fence.
Neither of us are natural gardeners.

Long ago in the moonlight of Trumpington
we stayed up feeding roots and spraying
leaf curl in the peach tree. You were gallant,
a poet at ten years old, your smile open,
loyally unheeding my neglect.

There are Belmondo lines of laughter now,
while your two daughters watch with admiration.
And those tomatoes grew plump and tangy,
as it turned out: undeserved gifts,
like stories from your newly fluent pen.

Bed

for a grandchild at six months

The summer garden breathes through my
window, baby Natasha. Untroubled on a pillow,
your eyelids in the rapid movement of dreams, you
learn the scent of my skin and hair,
the body warmth of this bed.

And what I'd wish you to inherit is
the sense of your pretty mother and

your father's brave heart, and grow to relish
the ordinary privilege of daylight
in their house of music and easy laughter.

Now let these words be a loving charm
against the fear of loneliness, and
under a cold moon, you may remember
this bundled duvet as somewhere once
familiar, where you came to no harm.

Amy Levy

Precocious, gifted girl, my nineteenth-century
voice of Xanthippe, I dreamed of you last night,
walking by the willows behind the Wren,
and singing to me of Cambridge and unhappiness.

'Listen, I am the first of my kind, and
not without friends or recognition,
but my name belongs with my family
in Bayswater, where the ghosts

of wealthy Sephardim line the walls,
and there I am alien because I sing.
Here, it is my name that makes me strange.
A hundred years on, is it still the same?'

Allegiance

We like to eat looking at boats. At night
in Jaffa harbour, the whole sea is alight
with glow worms of the local fisherman's floats.

My English friend has blue flirtatious eyes
and feels no danger. Her intrepid forbears
first explored, then colonised the planet.

Now over Yemenite eggplant and fried dough
we talk about the Roman exploitation
of Caesarea two thousand years ago

and find the history easy to agree.
Politics here and now are another matter.
The scared, open faces of the soldiers

look like oppressors to her, while my inheritance
– Kovno, Odessa, packing and running away –
makes me fear for them, as if they were sons.

So I can't share the privilege of guilt. Nor could
she taste the Hebrew of Adam in
the red earth here: the iron, salt and blood.

Rosemary in Provence

We stopped the Citroen at the turn of the lane,
because you wanted a sprig of blue rosemary
to take home, and your coat opened awkwardly

as you bent over. Any stranger would have
seen your frail shoulders, the illness
in your skin – our holiday on the Luberon

ending with salmonella –
but what hurt me, as you chose slowly,
was the delicacy of your gesture:

the curious child, loving blossom
and mosses, still eager
in your disguise as an old man.

Mirror

Mirror, mirror, what's going on?
A matron aunt or stubborn father
these days looks out of the mirror.
When I smile at them they are gone.

A pace behind the silvered glass
they wait like ghosts, though not so much
scary as shy, eager to touch
my present flesh with their own past.

Within my body is a thread
of which resemblance is the sign:
my story is not only mine
but an extension of the dead.

Prayer

The windows are black tonight. The lamp
at my bedside peering with its yellow
40 watt light can hardly make out the chair.
Nothing is stranger than the habit of prayer.

The face of God as seen on this planet
is rarely gentle: the young gazelle is food
for the predator; filmy shapes
that need little more than carbon and water,

evolve like patterns on Dawkins'
computer; the intricate miracles
of eye and wing respond to the same
logic. I accept the evidence.

God is the wish to live. Everywhere,
as carnivores lick their young with
tenderness, in the human struggle
nothing is stranger than the habit of prayer.

From
Gold

Gold

I

A wintry gold floods the bedroom this morning:
a January sun, drenching the air, alight
in a silk scarf, a yellow flare in the mirror.
I used to revel in the glitter of night,
but, over here, the dark has little glamour.

Let me introduce myself: Lorenzo da Ponte.
Mozart would smile to see me here in America
weighing out tea or measuring a yard
of plug tobacco. I have bolts of cloth,
salt pork in kegs, sewing thread, waxed cord.

My customers are cobblers or carters.
They offer lame horses and watery cider
instead of money; I must be content
to scratch a meagre living as a grocer.
It is a mask I wear, and I have spent

most of my life in one disguise or another.
Living on my wits – *Se vuol ballare,*
Signor Contino – like my Figaro,
but always more of an interloper.
Where did I find the nerve to put my toe

over the baroque threshold of the feudal?
My father lived in the stink of untreated
leather, without comfort or property,
hoping for nothing more than our survival.
He knew nothing of Tasso or Dante.

And so was spared the evil whispers
behind the jewelled hands of gorgeous
ladies in the Imperial Court.
In Europe, the children of tanners
do well to remain tanners.

I remember three Empires, but
what do I recall by now of Ceneda?
Disorder, hunger, urine, cats in
the streets and all the usual clobber
of poverty, shoeless children, dirt.

If there were any men with fat purses
in that ghetto north of Venice, my father
was not among them, poor man, confused
by many creditors, he was no usurer,
but rather harshly used.

Ceneda put a sibilance in my Italian,
although I never learnt the stoop of
the older generation, and women,
I soon noticed, liked my courteous
words, fine hands, and even

the stranger's darkness in my eyes.
Dove sono i bei momenti. Yes,
lovely creatures, ill used by their husbands,
were generous to me. You hear their voice
in my sad aria for the Countess,

Mozart transfigured in his garden music.
Dove sono i bei momenti? My pen
could race down pages, lickety-split,
writing of the unhappiness in women.
You will not find my words in Beaumarchais.

Here in Elizabethville, a girl with skin
of white milk and dimples, often
comes into my shop with a child
to collect her husband's medicine.
I know he bullies her. One day,

I saw a bruise under her eye. Before
my lips had framed the obvious question
her boy surprised me – *Mister, what happened
to your teeth?* She pulled him close
to hush him in his ear. I am a man

in late middle age, a little vain – toothless
or not – and scrupulously dressed.
I still walk upright, though I use a cane.
And briefly, I was tempted to confess
the flattering details of a scabrous story.

My Nancy was upstairs, however, making
her *cappelletti Bolognese*. So,
for all my rumoured immorality, not a
tender word was spoken, though
she might have listened like a Desdemona,

and perhaps my snubs and humiliations
would then have gained the spell of an adventure,
as if I had chosen to live on the run.
Just as the very dust of the air in
sunshine takes on the lustre of sequins.

3

The teeth? Well, I'll come to that story later.
There's a more serious matter, which still grates
in my flesh like seeds of dirt in an oyster.
I wanted to live with a bit of flash and brio,
rather than huddle behind ghetto gates.

It's not a question of faith. What I wanted to do
I knew as soon as I started to read Italian,
learnt on my own from torn books in the attic.
And only poetry could work the magic
of changing me into a European.

My mother died before I was five. My father,
too distressed to comfort anyone, found teachers
who were ignorant of Latin. I was not content
to be excluded from the opportunity of
being a child of the Enlightenment.

Far from getting answers to my questions,
my brother and I were often whipped.
As for scruples of my ancient religion,
I learnt little of those beyond the script
of the Hebrew language, though

a few sayings entered my imagination.
If I am not for myself, as Hillel has it,
*who will be for me? And if I am
only for myself, what am I? And if
not now, when?* He was a poet.

When I was fourteen, my father wished
to marry a Christian girl. The price
was the conversion of the whole family.
Knowing so little of what I was to enter,
I thought Christendom must be Paradise.

There were drums beating, cathedral bells,
halberdiers in ceremonial dress, the Feast
of the beheading of St John the Baptist,
when I who was born Emanuele
Conigliano became Lorenzo da Ponte.

I knelt down to become a citizen, and
shoved my origins out of my mind. I thought
if a little water purified my hand,
my spirit could flow into the main stream,
whatever earlier generations taught.

It seemed a gift of fortune unalloyed
when the same Bishop, whose name we'd taken,
put my brother and I in a seminary. Buoyed
up by reading Petrarch, Ovid, Horace,
I became so crazily studious

I had no time to chafe at celibate life.
My mentors, sadly, thought me too ambitious,
and mocked my first verses. Those who find
in my behaviour only desire for material good
miss out my schoolboy trust in all mankind.

4

Venice was water and sky, barges
of musicians on the Grand Canal,
perfumes, fans, a fever of carnival.
On my first visit there, I fell in love
with the whole city: the shops open,

till midnight, shopkeepers singing
as loudly as gondoliers. I lingered
in bookshops and in coffee houses
talking to men of letters. On my first visit,
I won the reputation of a wit.

The next, I had my purse of coins stolen
and didn't care, since I could see beggars
able to relish singers and lanterns.
Alas, I was to blame in staying on, for
when my father's leather shop went under,

he'd urged my brother and I into the Church
to train as priests – and I did not resist.
For someone of my temperament, that mask
was one, at least, that should have been rejected.
A priestly vow is dangerous, if neglected.

To begin with, venal sins aroused little
opprobrium as such. How I behaved
with girls was altogether commonplace.
Voi che sapete ... I was soon the slave
of Angiola, a ferocious beauty

who taught me all that was depraved
in pleasure, praising my precocity,
with delicate caresses, smiling to see
anxieties forgotten. She encouraged me
to think a little money might

keep our delicious nights alive for ever.
My friend Casanova, who was much colder,
more brutal – he devoured women like
sweetmeats – warned me her brother
was a well-known pimp but I took no notice

– Venice was a city of courtesans – though
sometimes glances that the two exchanged
held an affection something more than sibling.
I was too young, and did not want to know
what in the outcome had me half deranged.

So I joined their gambling in taverns.
Once a good hearted gondolier lent
me a few coins, and that won others, so
for a time I became Angiola's mascot.
The gift I gave back. And the rest we spent.

Now where, I wonder, did that fiction rise
that all my tribe are both wealthy and mean?
When on the Rialto, sometimes, I saw men
in beards wearing their gabardines,
with sallow faces, I lowered my eyes,

in case they read my stare as one that mocked.
They were old, and sad, and if there lurked
among them any single, vengeful Shylock,
he would not cherish any hope of justice
within the noble Christian courts of Venice.

Infatuated, dissolute, poor, at last
I tried on a new mask; that of magician.
And since Venetians put some trust
in alchemy, for a time I prospered,
as if I were a licensed conjuror,

though naturally no gold was ever made.
The Church still took no interest in me.
It was as if I'd simply found a trade.
The role was one I might even have played
for longer, if one afternoon I had not

found my sweet Angiola in our bed
with two men, entertained lasciviously.
Challenged, she threw an inkpot at my head.
I had no choice. I picked up a few clothes.
That very hour, without much dignity

I left the city in a jealous temper,
making for Treviso, where I could
earn some money as a Latin teacher,
while writing a few poems on the need
for human beings to behave as brothers.

My politics at the time were innocent.
I did not imagine much original
in what I wrote, almost as exercise.
The morals I approved were Roman, decent;
but looked seditious to an Abbot's eyes.

And I was in the Church. All of my past
actions were examined in a new light.
I stood accused as gambler, fornicator,
adulterer and rapist, though that last
for my own pride I must deny.

Those poems brought me to the attention
of the Venetian Senate. The Inquisition
was soon investigating my conversion.
I did not stay to argue the position,
but left sweet Venice quickly for Trieste.

5

And what to do next? My brother's income
was, I well knew, committed to support
my father and the family. From now on,
the Church banned my employment as a teacher.
Was I condemned to living as a con man?

Not my intention, but I'd have to busk it.
I was outside Venetian jurisdiction, but
the Church has a long arm, as well I knew,
and even to earn my bread I dared not risk it.
You cannot always recognise

the good news from the bad. I might,
without that incident, have spent
my whole life in a dingy backwater.
Instead, it was to Dresden that I went
to see an old friend, who was Court poet

to the opera. He knew I had some talent,
though while I hung around he did
little to further it. It was only
the morning I was on my way
the fellow seemed suddenly to relent,

as if sure then of no awkward demands.
He scribbled a few lines to Salieri
in Vienna: 'Do for him everything
that you would do for me.'
And with that letter a new life began.

6

Enough. You want to hear about Mozart.
How did he live? Who were his favourite women?
Did he have any secret habits, stuff
he put in Tokay, or snorted with his snuff?
As if what genius does for recreation

has much to tell us about what he is.
I can only say: I loved the man,
and if you wonder what I had in common
– apart from laughter and frivolities –
with such a genius, famous since he was six,

I'd say: though I was a late starter
we rapidly gained the same enemies
– Casti, for instance, syphilitic, burring
through the wreckage of his nose –
as both of us hustled on the peripheries.

In Vienna, nothing counts but rank.
A Baron with a house in Herrengasse,
and all his land in hock, still keeps a gig
painted with family insignia, his wig
is well cut, and his clothes elegant.

That's Empire for you. And always, at the centre,
toadies will prosper more than any talent.
Which is not to say I couldn't flatter
but even at the height of my acceptance,
the snobbish flunkeys always had my measure.

Still, there were pretty milliners, dressed
in feathers, cafés on the Graben.
At first, I took up lodging with a tailor
near Taborgasse, where the market stalls
sold trinkets, hot potato cakes, and shawls,

from GOLD   119

and settled in, before taking my letter
to Salieri in the First District. Naturally
I greeted him at once as an Italian,
while he read over what I'd brought, with caution.
I didn't mention my priestly career,

but said I had a Bishop as a godfather.
On some matters, I had to stay alert,
if not evasive, since the Emperor's mother
in her lifetime had allowed no Jews, convert
or other, any place in her Vienna.

Salieri introduced me to the Emperor;
I was appointed to the Italian Theatre,
and on that stage discovered my true home.
The make believe delighted me at once:
I loved the candle starlight, painted domes,

the filmy, shimmering clothes, and feathery wings
which transformed actors into gods and kings.
That said, the only people there who prosper
in opera houses are the leading singers.
They hold the rest to ransom: scene shifters,

tailors, extras, engineers, composers
and poets always bottom of the pile.
Salieri I thought witty and versatile,
but my first opera, let me confess,
– with his music – was not a success.

The Emperor was kind about my failure,
encouraged me to try my luck again;
when the next went well, he whispered
to me: *Abbiamo vinto*. So I was in favour.
For a time, could use green porcelain

to eat my breakfast, sit on lacquered
white chairs with goats' feet, wear
an ankle length coat of Chinese silk,
and be a guest in the Imperial palace,
though I might well fear poison in the chalice.

When I was ill, I warmed my bed with embers
in a copper pan, drank claret and madeira.
I worked for anyone: Martin y Soler,
Martini, Storace. Whoever asked.
I learnt my trade as I performed the task.

Is it a serious art to write libretti
when so few people listen to the words?
Those who found me glib, would often say
I did no more than *translate* poetry,
and steal the shape of better writers' plays.

Beaumarchais himself was rather kinder.
He said *The Marriage of Figaro*, cut
into our version, was a miracle, and that
to turn a five act play into an opera
was of itself to make a new drama.

When Mozart wanted to set *Figaro*, the play
was banned in Austria, I dared suggest
I knew exactly what could be hacked out.
And Emperor Joseph let us have our way.
It was a risk, but somehow I had guessed

that in that chance lay immortality. I changed
Figaro's first name, for superstition:
Beaumarchais had him as Emanuel,
which was my own name before baptism.
I wanted no gossip about my religion

– as if that would ever dwindle away.
There were many around us who were jealous,
not of my skills, of course, but Mozart's genius,
and they included Salieri, my first patron.
It was stupid of me, then, to start a liaison

with a singer that he thought belonged to him.
In those days I was rash, and handsome,
with all my teeth. Ah yes. I promised you
that story. I have never been quite sure
how much what followed had to do with him.

A girl where I lodged had dismissed her lover,
praising my good looks. I hardly knew her,
or the rejected lover, save as a surgeon,
till I met him in a coffee shop, and mentioned
one of my gums might have to be lanced.

'Cut?' he said. 'No need of that.
For a sequin I will rid you of the trouble.'
When he returned he had a blue glass bottle.
'Put this on your gums,' he said, 'with a cloth.'
And so I did, and thanked him for his skill.

My nature at the time was not suspicious.
I was putting on the lotion with a placid
hand, obedient to instructions, without
a thought of any danger, when
my maid screamed out: 'Jesus, that's nitric acid!'

– she often used the stuff for washing clothes.
I did not doubt her, rinsed my mouth at once
with vinegar and milk. The harm was done.
And in a few days my gums were wax.
On the left side my teeth dropped one by one.

7

They didn't take to *Figaro* in Vienna.
We had to wait for Prague. One day,
along the Graben, I met Casanova.
I was feeling low, since hearing that my brother
– abler than me and far more virtuous –

had fallen ill and died. I cursed whatever
powers muddle up God's justice.
My friend and I fell into each other's arms.
Although we'd quarrelled long ago in Venice,
I never wished the fellow any harm.

We dined that evening with a pretty dancer
and La Ferrarese, an opera diva
of whom you will hear more. In Grinzing
we ate roast goose and drank champagne together.
Soon after, I was afire with *Don Giovanni,*

and put the plot of it in front of Mozart.
He liked it, and I've never written faster.
I kept awake by taking Seville snuff,
a girl of sixteen sitting close enough
for me to fondle, when my ink ran dry.

And then it was a tranquil Prague October.
I recall autumn leaves, and birdshell skies;
in an old farmhouse Mozart and Constanze
stayed – I have never heard such birdsong –
while I lodged opposite The Three Lions.

We were still doing re-writes that week,
so I was involved in the rehearsals,
but Mozart would not write the overture.
The more we pleaded, the more he was playful.
At last, we tricked him into the Bertramka

and locked him in upstairs with his piano.
Seeing us through the window, he spoke
fretfully of being left alone. We passed up wine
and baked meat, begging him resign
himself to work, and then he took it as a joke,

and with relief we heard the first notes
of the score. A coachman took me home.
That night I walked about the city,
enjoying Prague, and gossiping with Czechs
whose late night badinage was wry and witty.

Their theatre goers favour the dramatic.
They have a legend of an ancient monster
haunting the stones of the Jews' cemetery,
but they are my ghosts, the dead who lie there,
and, if unquiet, they don't frighten me.

It was my touch to have the father's statue
return for his revenge, though Mozart
blenched at it. He felt some guilt, I knew,
for disobedience of his own father. I had
no fear of mine rising out of Hell

since he was still alive and short of money,
no apparition needed to remind.
In *Stavovské Divadlo*, that anxiety
quickly dropped out of my mind. It was
the prettiest Theatre I had seen.

And at the first performances, I gasped
to see the audience in their finery
and hear the bustle; I had never grasped
what listening to applause would mean to me.
I knew they'd loved our *Figaro*, of course,

but had not heard the clapping for myself
or felt elation stirring in my blood. Seeing
my own libretto, bound in gold paper
sold outside at 40 crowns a copy
seemed to authenticate my whole being.

8

The dialogue, the counterpoint, the melodies:
Là ci darem la mano was my favourite.
Meanwhile composers, still using my libretti,
began to mock my ignorance of music,
and often said, you cannot trust a man,

who cannot even play a simple piano,
and makes his living out of writing opera.
He speaks too cleverly, and so it is
that foolish women throw themselves at him.
La Ferrarese, say, who played Susanna

in *Marriage of Figaro*, during its revival.
She was my mistress, yes, although
she brought me to my knees more by her
singing than her beauty, her contralto
voice, teasing as well as pleasing.

I knew the substance of her reputation
– her jealousy, her street violence –
but, warned against the association
because she had so many enemies,
I became even more her partisan,

and gave her parts for which she was
unsuited. Meanwhile, many voices
spoke viciously of my collaboration:
in *Così fan tutte*. It was a gentle variation
on the old story of inconstant women.

Mozart's angelic harmonies transformed
my wicked plot, but there were moralists
who found me cynical, and warned
I should not be indulged inside the Court.
Salieri arranged most of the slanders.

Perhaps it was support of La Ferrarese
made me so unpopular? Her song
was out of fashion, and she herself was old
when our love ended. Something went wrong.
And soon the new Emperor, Leopold,

looked on me with so much disfavour
I had to leave the comforts of Vienna
for London, marriage and financial ruin.
But let me say, my bride was not the problem.
My Nancy had amazing acumen,

as well as youth and beauty. In my English
troubles – with an unscrupulous producer
whose notes I'd signed in rather foolish
fashion – Nancy was much shrewder.
She ran a coffee house and kept the profit

in her own name, until we sailed away
from Europe, debts and prejudice –
she was another convert, by the way –
to a New World over the stormy seas
where nobody recalls our histories.

9

To speak now as an enlightened ghost,
my end was better than you might suppose.
In New York, in a bookshop once, I met
by chance a man who loved Italian poets.
When he discovered what I knew by heart

he introduced me to his wealthy friends.
And even as Nancy and I entered society,
the Italian Opera with my *Don Giovanni*
was crossing the Atlantic. When it arrived,
I found that my celebrity revived.

My Nancy became a renowned hostess,
who carried herself with grace and, since
she spoke four languages, easily impressed
our new admirers. As for me,
I taught the treasures of Italian poetry.

Poor Mozart was so much less fortunate.
My only sadness is to think of him, a pauper,
lying in his grave, while I became
Professor of Italian literature.
Nobody living can predict their fate.

I moved across the cusp of a new age,
to reach this present hour of privilege.
On this earth, luck is worth more than gold.
Politics, manners, morals all evolve
uncertainly. Best then to be bold.

Living Room

How can we make friends before one of us dies
if you quarrel with two fingers in your ears,
like a child? Things won't come out right now.
You think I don't love you. I won't argue.
Your angry sadness stings me into tears.
I think of your old mac, smelling of chemicals,
leant against long ago in the 'Everyman' queue,

when you offered me those tender early
films that made our lips tremble, or else
the forgiven boy in the forest of Ravel's opera,
more touching to me than your verbal
skills or passion for the genius of gesture
in crayon, mime, *commedia dell'arte.*
It's love we miss, and cannot bear to lose.

I know you would much prefer I choose
intelligence to prize, but that has
always had its down side, your words
so often cut me down to size, I wonder
if some accident removed me first, whether
my writing days would count as evidence
that in my loss was little real to miss.

The likeliest end is that the bay tree left
to my attention, withers on the window sill,
and moths lay eggs in the lentils, while
still hurt by memories of you as gentle, I'll
look into a monitor for comfort, and cry
aloud at night in the hope somewhere
your lonely spirit might hang on and care.

Paradise

Even the sad music from the car radio is glamorous
this morning, as I take the curve up the hill.
The sun glitters on rainy streets
like a shoal of herrings in water,
this early March tingles my blood
as yellow touches the strands of a willow:
a freedom intoxicating and dangerous.

No one knows where I am. No one
cares what I do. It's alarming
to be untethered as a kite slipped from
a child's hand, and then blown past
this high street of shop windows: Monsoon,
French Connection, Waterstones.

The last gives me pause. I wonder
whether it was cowardice or duty
denied me this pleasure so long,
to take comfort from the name on a book spine
or italic under a photo, while the blood
of my life found a pulse only in song.

In Praise of Flair

That whole wet summer, I listened to Louis Armstrong.
Imagined him arriving in New York after Funky Butt
dance halls, wearing hick clothes: those
high top shoes with hooks, and long
underwear down to his socks.

Thought of him shy in a slick, new band, locked
for two weeks reading the part he was set,
until the night when Bailey on clarinet
took over an old song. Then Louis' horn
rose in harsh, elated notes,

of phrases he'd invented on riverboats
and ratty blues tonks, using all the sinews
of his face and muscle of his tongue.
And what delights me now,
is when he grinned to thank

the crowd that stood to clap, and saw
slyly from the corner of his eye
all the stingy players in the band
were sitting motionless, their tribute
only an astonished sigh.

After La Traviata

She calls *Too late* from her bed, and in fury
I feel the hot salt spilling out of my eyes,
as if her need to love undermined all witness.
One great cry, and we forget his mistrust,
her jewels sold in secret to pay their bills;
and lament only for happiness lost.

Yet even without the blackmail and bullying
of the father's intervention, Violetta's surrender
speaks of a passion foreign to our age, when
people are supposed to move off for their own good;
and friends to chivvy them out of such obsessions.
Why should she spend herself to the last cough of blood?

The tears give another answer. Looking around,
in the ENO audience, I see women weeping
on every side, as if such commitment arouses
a profound longing; we may refuse to be sacrificed,
but respond to the fiction, are betrayed
in the music, and not only in opera houses.

Casualty

A green computer called George is reading
my vital signs through a peg on an index finger.
I try to understand the bleeps, while the Ibo nurse
chuckles and gives his rusty stand a kick:
'This one, he's unreliable old thing.'

Four a.m. She leaves, and then it's lonely.
Even George has gone now, though eight leads
are still attached to my chest and legs. I'm
knackered, but I can't sleep on the trolley
and there's nothing here to look at but a shelf

of cardboard piss pots and an oxygen mask,
the bin for contaminated spikes, and a
red button to be pushed in asthmatic spasm.
Impatient for daylight, tossing in my cot,
thoughts rattle in my head: I want

my ordinary life back. What
a mistake to let an ambulance
carry me off to this wretched ward.
There may be nothing much wrong.
That sudden hope rises in me like birdsong.

Jeopardy

All year I've watched the velvet glow
of your happiness, seen you flow
towards him, while he bathes in your spirit;
a glittering exchange of tongue and wit.
I've known what you wanted most was
the risk of giving without calculation.

Now he consumes your pleasure along
with grapes, tree fungus, red nectar,
and since he is no ordinary sailor,
takes the island for his own, as he
receives your enchanted songs.
Calypso, Calypso,

What he gives in return is splendour:
partly his own, and partly the mirror
in which you perceive your own beauty:
the sum of everything he ever loved.
Relishing the energy of his self-concern,
you have already forgiven his onward journey.

From
Talking to the Dead

Winter

The clock's gone back. The shop lights spill
over the wet street, these broken streaks
of traffic signals and white headlights fill
the afternoon. My thoughts are bleak.

I drive imagining you still at my side,
wanting to share the film I saw last night,
– of wartime separations, and the end
when an old married couple reunite –

*You never did learn to talk and find the way
at the same time*, your voice teases me.
Well, you're right, I've missed my turning,
and smile a moment at the memory,

always knowing you lie peaceful and curled
like an embryo under the squelchy ground,
without a birth to wait for, whirled
into that darkness where nothing is found.

Bremerhaven

Christmas in Bremerhaven. Every twig sheathed
in transparent ice like tubes of glass, each breath
steam as it left our lips.
I did not want to go to the fair.

You would have liked to poke through toys
even in freezing rain, and relished the stalls
of rich cakes, bought some German games,
but I did not want to be there.

Then, in a wooden booth where we took shelter,
my son and I drank *Glühwein* and spoke of you.
He was still angry about childhood memories,
and, as he spoke, suddenly, you were there,

– one-off, sardonic and obstreperous –
as if we had conjured your hot presence
to stand for a moment solidly between us,
before you dissolved back into the air.

Beds

Last night I wondered where you had found to sleep.
You weren't in bed. There was no one in your chair.

Through every window the white, full moon glared.
I walked into the garden, shivering:

'Where are you, my darling? You will catch cold.'
Waking, I let the daytime facts unfold.

Mackintosh

Your spirit comes to me in a mackintosh
scented with volatile esters from the lab.
No one remembers you now as I remember:
your voice still shy, your sentences unfinished.
We were living in two rooms over the bridge
somewhere in Mill Road with mice in the kitchen.

I have never been so happy, you told me when
your grant came through, and then began
to sit all night in the basement of Free School Lane
watching a fraction collector,
muffled up in the same mackintosh,
which was grimed at the pockets

and worn with the belt twisted. This you flung
over the end of our bed in the early morning.
We were clumsy, unfastidious, tender.
Your spirit comes to me now
in a mackintosh to remind me how
easily we loved when we were young.

Home

When was it you took up that second stick,
and began to walk like a cross country skier?
Your glide developed its own politics.
Last July, you were able to stretch over
like an acrobat, to oil the garden table.
The patio faced south. It was high summer.

Coffee and grapefruit was the breakfast ritual,
or boiled eggs eaten from blue terracotta.
Our paradise, you called it, like a *gîte*
we might have chosen somewhere in Provence.
Neither of us understood you were in danger.
Not even when we called the ambulance:

you'd been inside so many hospitals,
ticking your menus, shrugging off jabs and scans
talking unstoppably to visitors –
your long crippling made you bitterly clever.
Humped on your atoll, and awash with papers
you often argued like an angry man.

This time, however, you were strangely gentle.
Your face lit up as soon as I arrived;
smiling, you shooed the nurses out, and said
Now go away, I'm talking to my wife.
You liked it, when I brought myself to say
seeing you was the high point of my day.

The nurses, pushed for time, hauled you about
and fixed the bed without much ceremony.
You spoke of *home*, as if you were ET,
and wanted me to fetch you in the car – as
I would have, if the staff nurse had concurred.
Darling, they brought you in like a broken bird.

Your shoulder blades were sharp beneath your skin,
a high cheekbone poignant against the pillow.
Yet neither of us spoke a word of death.
My love, you whispered, *I feel so safe with you.*
That Monday, while I phoned, you waited loyally
for my return, before your last breath.

Immortality

If I believed in an old-fashioned Paradise,
then you, my love, would still be talking in it.
There would be blue sky and a few clouds
seen through stone arches, as in
Raphael's *School of Athens*, with Diogenes
sprawled on the steps, and Plato in the likeness of da Vinci.
You could pursue them with your eager questions –
as you once challenged speakers at LSE.

It's not that I hope to find you there
myself, more that I cannot bear
it should be true as once you said:
We think. And learn to understand a bit.
And then we're dead…

A Match

You hated swank.

Even in flowers
you did not like flamboyance
preferring small blue
petals of rosemary
to flags and peonies.

I liked a bit of flash,
glittery clothes, immodest
dancing, some euphoria
always with Dorothy Parker's
knowledge of disaster.

All our worst faults we shared:
disorder, absentmindedness, neglect.
You asked me once: *How*
did you get away with it?
before concluding harshly:

You must have been a tank.

Skin

There was a time *before* we met as well
as this inexorable *after*. If I had not

found you, who would I have been?
A woman who could dance a stylish tango

fretted with too much wanting – sex, success –
spoilt, self-seeking, and a little shallow

distrusting what I could not understand. There were
so many men I cannot list them all.

Some I abandoned, some abandoned me.
One I loved well gave me a diamond –

I often wondered what happened to him –
Then you became the skin of all I am.

Flame

There must be something I still hope to find.
Honour, perhaps. I do not look for love.

We never said goodbye, though I remember
whispering to you in the Royal Free,

'You do know, I have loved you all my life?'
with a quick nod and smile your only answer.

Once you described me as *a natural spinster*,
meaning a loner, happiest on my own;

you knew that was not so. Once home from
hospital, you called me *wife* and *mother* –

that last was what you wished.
Will you take these poems from me now

as if they were Akhmatova's snowdrops,
or a flame in a clay dish?

Another Anniversary

Today is your birthday. There is cool sunshine.
Fig leaves and roses cover the wooden fence.
What happiness can I wish you in your death?

Here is the garden that I made for us
though you saw only the winter shape
of a weeping crab apple and a bare plum,

it was my offering, and you received it so;
but most of what we work at disappears.
Little we worry over has importance.

The greedy and the generous have the same end.
The dead know nothing of what we say to them.
Still, in that silence let me write: *dear friend*.

A Pebble on Your Grave

It's easy to love the dead.
Their voices are mild. They don't argue.
Once in the earth, they belong to us faithfully.

But do they forgive us?
Our crabby failure to understand
their complaints, our manifest indignation

at words of blame. Once, I remember
you broke off some angry
exchange to say unhappily:

I don't want your silly grief
after I'm dead, it's now
I need your pity.

Widow's Necklace

Friends try my stories on their teeth or
with a match: are they plastic or amber?

My children say I must have forgotten
how I used to turn to them so very often

repeating your words and begging reassurance.
Why should I now recall a loving presence?

But so I do: my story as a wife
is threaded on the string of my own life,

and when I touch those beads, I still remember
your warm back as we slept like spoons together.

Wheelchair

We've travelled on a bumboat on the green South China seas,
seen papaya, dates and coconuts in crotches of the trees
and in hawker centres Singapore keep quietly policed
eaten hundred year old eggs and fishbrains wrapped in bamboo leaf.

but the most surprising feature of the perils we have passed
is you've travelled in a wheelchair with your left leg in a cast.
Most people would have had more sense, but we were both
                                      surprised
to find it rather soothing. And one day we surmised:
you needed an attention that I hardly ever pay
while I enjoyed the knowledge that you couldn't get away.

Now the generator flickers far inland in Campuhan
and we lie inside our cottage cooled remotely by a fan,
or take a bath among the ferns and tall hibiscus trees.
Green rice grows in the paddy fields, we pick the coffee beans.
And outside, parked and ready, sits the chair that takes you round
to explore in a contentment that we've only rarely found.

1997

From *Scattering*

I

In the lands of Sepharad, on the River Tagus:
a town the colour of biscuit, a long horizon,
smooth, bare mountains, and beyond
the desert and a white sliver of moon.

It is the limestone city of Toledo, where
the Jews settled after Jerusalem
– silversmiths, traders, basket-makers, scholars –
and Spain at first was happy to receive them.

In a Golden Age of restored hope:
houses were built with fountains in the courtyard;
men in their book-lined studies were translators
who brought the Greeks through Arabic to Europe.

But when they had to leave, with frightened eyes,
they bartered a house for a donkey,
a vineyard for a wheelbarrow,
and nicknames followed them, like police spies.

2

And those who did not leave?
They turned to the Holy Cross,
though some lit candles on a Friday night
without remembering why,

and cooked in oil rather than lard;
others became fervent New Christians,
and married into the best families;
until the Inquisition began to inquire

more urgently into their old habits,
– for instance, if they did not light a fire
on Saturdays in a cold winter –
Neighbours gave evidence against the rich.

Most admitted their sins under torture, as
people will, and some were brought to blame
fellow *conversos* for their practices.
It did not help them to escape the flames.

Nor did the ignorant suffer any less.
Read how Elvira del Campo pleaded,
as they broke her arms, only to understand:
Tell me what I have done that I may confess.

4

Not so easy in the lands of Ashkenaz.
Winter. Snow. Trees. An acrid smell
of gunpowder in the wind.
Not many Jews in Vienna's First District:

bankers paid a heavy tax for the privilege.
Those with beards and caftans came for the Fairs
and, when times were hard, they set up
market stalls near Leopoldstrasse

selling trinkets, second-hand goods or
potato cakes with sour pickles.
Emancipation let them be newspaper editors,
scribblers and soldiers. In a Hapsburg Empire

stretching through Budapest into Galicia
for all the ambiguities, Jews were loyal.
Assimilation would have been
honourable then, if it had been possible.

Let us not speak of Germany.
The best loved, the most murderous…

5

When Herman Melville visited Palestine
he saw a desolate landscape bleached
like bones, no moss, just naked stones
with lime ash in between them.

The Jewish stores then only sold rice,
or dingy looking sugar and dried fish.
Pale faced women were gnarled
as olive trees and carried sickly children.

Everywhere he saw sand and cactus.
Only the Bedou riding in from the desert
in flowing robes on camels stirred his blood.
Otherwise the land was not glamorous

hardly inviting settlement, even
for those caught in Kishinyov, still less
in Western Europe, before
the conviction of Captain Dreyfus.

6

I remember the broken bodies aboard
rotting ships turned back by the British:
how the young swam for the shore,
and the old preferred to drown.

I drank green tea with my Moroccan lover,
looking across barbed wire in Jerusalem.
At the end of that street were Jordanian guns.
No one expected Israel to survive.

In Gesher HaZiv I was covered
with mosquito bites and afraid of spiders
living in the banana plants, but at night
we danced and I wore Yemenite silver.

Five wars later, Yehuda Amichai
told me in his house in Yemin Moshe:
I am completely unapologetic. Why
should I feel guilty for being here

writing poems and still hoping for peace?
I had to confess that in London, the same people
who once sent their children to work on kibbutzim
have begun to question Israel's right to exist.

London

for Natasha

A full ginger moon hangs in the garden.
On this side of the house there are no stars.
When I go to bed, I like to soothe myself with
streetlights, lit windows and passing cars.

When my grandchild comes to sleep over
I find we share the same preference.
She doesn't want to draw the curtains either.
I like to look out on my town, my London...

Have you seen London from above? she asks me.
It's like a field of lights. And her grey eyes widen.
Her eight-year-old spirit is tender as blossom.
Be gentle to her now, ferocious London.

From
Cities

Migrations

1

In late March, birds from the Gambia,
white throat warblers, who wintered in
the branches of a feathery acacia;
Mandelstam's goldfinch; pink foot
geese from the Arctic. All
arrive using the stars, along
flyways old as Homer and Jeremiah.

2

Avian immigration is down this year,
but humans still have reasons to move on,
the usual chronicle of poverty, enemies,
or ominous skies the colour of tobacco.
They arrive in London with battered luggage,
and eyes dark as black cherries

holding fast to old religions
and histories, remembering
the shock of being hunted in the streets,
the pain at leaving their dead
in broken cemeteries, their resilience
hardwired as birds' skill in navigation.

On the Jubilee line, a black woman
has the profile of a wood carving from Benin.
In Willesden Green, *Polskie delikatesy*, or a grocer
piling up African vegetables. An English woman
buys hot ginger and white radish: the filigree
of migration, symbiosis, assimilation.

All my grandparents came from Odessa
a century ago, spoke little English,
and were doubtless suspect as foreigners
– probably anarchist or Bolshevik –
very likely to be dreaming of bombs.
It is never easy to be a stranger,

to be split between loneliness
and disloyalty, to be impatient
with dogma, yet still distrusted
in a world which prefers to be secular.
When I listen to the gaiety of Klezmer,
I understand why migrants like ghettos.

These people come from desperate countries
where flies walk over the faces of sick children,
and even here in Britain the luckless
will find gangmasters to arrange
work in mudflats as cockle pickers.
Why should they care my ancestors

had a long history of crossing borders,
when I am settled now after all those journeys?
And why do I want to make common cause
with them anyway? Only because I remember
how easily the civil world turns brutal.
If it does, we shall have the same enemies.

Cambridge, 1949

Look, how she teeters in a tight skirt
on high heels over the cobbled street,
past Heffers' gabled windows and knobbly glass,
the music of wartime dance bands still inside her –
what does she know of madrigals and choirs,
my adolescent self, in her first term?
She dreams of Soho clubs and Raymond Chandler.

Dismissing girls in tweedy clothes as dowdy,
she does not recognise the family names
connected into webs of social power; altogether
too unworldly to be a Marrano,
she says grace at High Table as a Scholar,
giggling, over wet lettuce and beetroot,
unaware of any reserve around her.

Yet as she reads in her Newnham room the metaphysical
poets claim her, and she enters
the Christian centuries with Donne and Herbert,
filled with an unexpected terror.
What if it were all true? The angels
on the shore, the judgement,
the dismissal and her secular world denied?

What if this present were the world's last night?
The paradise of leaf dust and wood smoke
would vanish in the darker truth behind.
Unprotected by her own rituals
or any reading in the Sciences, she is caught
in a history told by eloquent strangers:
she prays alongside Gerard Manley Hopkins,

until a Fulbright student from New York
rescues her with mockery, and
lends her Pound's miraculous *Cathay*
which staggers her with the sad,

erotic beauty of an ancient culture
while he with skilful fingers,
teaches her in the shade of willow trees
how to explore further outside the syllabus.

Piaf in Babraham

The pin is loose that holds the climbing rose.
It crackles on the glass. I stare outside
at a single wet goat with oblong eyes:
bemused – a young wife and mother,
beyond the Gogs – and my own story over.

The bole and branches of the trees are smooth
– like water pipes – in sodium light.
The pop and bubble of children's
television rises up the stairs.
I scribble, while a voice reaches into me,

Edith Piaf, and the songs she chose, of failed
loves, loneliness, poverty.
I long for her Paris streets, and the glamour
of a woman who never had safety
to lose – the thin child with a monstrous voice

rattling centimes in a hat – those walls of mirrors
in grand restaurants – the Dietrich eyebrows
– even the drug pallor. All of it was her choice,
a tiny woman in a black dress,
with an audience ready to watch her collapse on stage.

Rien, je ne regrette rien. While I, in bland
everyday disorder, listen
to the soaring triumph in her voice, knowing
she has only earned that elation, because
she learned to sell her ordinary life for applause.

A Dream of Prague

i.m. Miroslav Holub

Prague is a city of dreams without sleep:
Franz Kafka looking
at a whore near Zeltnergasse,
a lady in white silk
in the Kinsky Palace, shadows
on the Karlsbrücke,
ancient street lamps, wooden apostles
like sinister toys,
circling the astronomical clock.

Yet where else shall I think of you now
but in this city? Perhaps
when Havel was in the Castle behind
red and blue toy soldiers;
or in sunshine, with loud blackbirds on the hill
below the Summer Palace.
Mozart first heard his *Don Giovanni* cheered
in this golden Opera House,
and here it was we met you, looking relaxed,

not as in London or Cambridge, where
your eyes were always
hooded and cautious, a dapper-suited irony
beneath your courteous
reluctance to meet émigré friends,
your chance to travel
linked to nude mice and scientific papers
– not that wild carnival
of poetry: paradox and pepper.

In Prague, then, with casual euphoria,
– President now of the very
Writers' Union which once banned your poetry –
you led us to applaud

Jiří Menzel, the impudent director of
Closely Observed Trains,
wearing canvas sneakers in the Hotel Adria.
We ate in an Art Deco café,
green marble and mosaic restored.

Your enemies now were, chiefly, alternative medicine,
astrology and other superstitions,
and your face was alight with inspired mockery.
We shared in the amusement.
So why did we return home edgy and sad?
Three weeks later,
a Czech friend rang to tell us you were dead,
your witty spirit
sailing off into the starry darkness
over the Belvedere.

Jerusalem

I

Your stones hold the glow of a June sun
until the desert night drops
a dark blue cloak over the streets

abruptly, as always in the Levant.
When I saw you first,
barbed wire threaded your heart,

and the clarity of your stars pierced me –
like an ancient tribal God.
I sold back all my silver trinkets

so I could wander the narrow alleys
with your white dust
in my sandals for a few days longer,

drink mint tea with my Moroccan lover
under Jordanian guns before
I left for rainy London and the man I married.

2 Abu Tor

We flew together, after the Six Day War,
– with an unfamiliar salt on our lips –
to visit Arieh Sachs, in Abu Tor
above the stone strewn valley of Cedron,
whose waters lead to the Valley of Hinnom,

supposedly the scene of the Last Judgement.
Arieh was holding a drinks party
fired by the peculiar astonishment,
of a boy who has taken on the school bully,
and floored him with an unexpected blow.

We argued until it was dawn with poet
conscripts: about courage and ghettos,
Warsaw and Sobibor. We talked
of peace, the loss of friends
and the dangerous energy men find in war.

Nobody spoke of Victory with elation,
or pretended local hatreds had gone away.
At first light, we set off along Nablus road
for the American Colony hotel
a Pasha's palace, where the journalists stay.

3

In Mishkenot Sha'ananim twenty years on
at the time of the first *intifada*
Amichai advised us sensibly:

Yes, go into the Old City
but not too often, and not
for long. When the shutters

begin to come down, remember
the shopkeepers are also afraid of gunmen.
So don't barter after you hear the bell.

4

In Mahane Yehuda, a few old Russian men are
playing *shesh besh* in the courtyard.

I am alone, here for a festival,
shivering in a light coat.

April is often cold in Jerusalem
But that's not why.
I met my old boyfriend
which was disappointing.

But that's not it. This time I saw Jerusalem
was no longer a secular city,

but part of the fanatic Middle East.
And I was frightened. Would the Lord protect her?

5 Postscript, London

Rain in August, and the rolling news
   shows rubble in Lebanon,
      and journalists fired up

by a war which plays better than the World Cup
   for adrenaline, raw excitement
      and indignation,

against Israel mainly, which is safely at a distance –
　　like Czechoslovakia in the thirties –
　　　　while London is confused on its fault line,

afraid tectonic plates may shift again, and
　　bring another day, as red as hatred
　　　　and white as death.

A flick of silver high in clear sky.
　　We look up and imagine:
　　　　Blood. Bone. Brain. Breath.

Dizzy in Westminster

Glossy black ringlets, blistering waistcoats, silver buckled shoes.
Where did you get the nerve for such flamboyance?
Not from your bookish father, skull-capped and scholarly,
whose anger with his Synagogue released you
into the gentile world, a baptised Jew.

Always in debt, and eager for renown,
only literary fame and a witty tongue gave you
entry to river parties and heady dinners
where politicians ate swans stuffed with truffles,
and married women readily became your tutors.

How did you bewitch those stolid gentlemen
of the shires to choose you for a leader?
Baptism did not make you less a Jew,
cartoonists mocked your aquiline profile
and drooping lip. But Parliament was your theatre.

Across the Dispatch Box, Gladstone
disliked your eloquence and found you
slippery, your talent opportunist –
while you thought him a prig. Let us
confess your policy imperialist,

your cleverest foreign deals somehow
congruent with your own extravagance.
Yet courage trumps all and demands tribute.
You flattered, entertained, but never cringed.
And that, dear Earl of Beaconsfield, I salute.

Christmas Day in Willesden Green

for my autistic grandchild

At fourteen, his eyes are dark as wood resin,
his hair red-gold; he is an elf-child
with delicate lips, and pale, unblemished skin.
The scented candles and the roasted goose
with apples in its throat don't interest him.
He flicks a dangled string and sets it loose

snatches a cracker biscuit, shaking off
the smoked fish, and then smiles suddenly
as if amused by some mischievous thought
growing out of a landscape I can't reach,
the unknown pathways lying under speech.
On these cold Christmas windows, heavy rain

begins, like the crackle of crumpled cellophane,
or an untuned radio; while Johnny remains soundless,
like a small bird gathering twigs and loam,
completely absorbed in his own business:
gold wrapping paper and coloured ribbons
are the treasures he brings to his sofa home.

It is the first year in seven the whole family
has eaten with him; we have feared his wild
behaviour and forgotten his misfortune,
as if that pain belonged to other people. Now he is mild,
we relax in noise and wine. Is he bewildered
among so many strangers, or reconciled?

Long Life

Late summer. Sunshine. The eucalyptus tree.
It is a fortune beyond any deserving
to be still *here*, with no more than everyday worries,
placidly arranging lines of poetry.

I consider a stick of cinnamon
bound in raffia, finches
in the grass, and a stubby bush
which this year mothered a lemon.

These days I speak less of death
than this miracle of survival. I am
no longer lonely, not yet frail, and
after surgery, recognise each breath

as a favour. My generation may not be
nimble but, forgive us,
we'd like to hold on, stubbornly
content – even while ageing.

From
Portraits

The Gamble

i.m. Sylvia Plath (1932–1963)

The woman in the mirror swimming
towards you like a terrible fish
never made landfall. Look upon this fin.
Observe the lines the scars the teeth the skin.
I am old as you will never be.

Your life was shorter than Mozart's or Pushkin's.
I remember living through the humiliation
you were too proud to bear, and now to imagine
the motive for your dying troubles me – was it
your poems that demanded that last gesture?

I honour your carbon-paper skies
typed through with stars, those winter trees
dissolving in their blotting-paper clouds.
You threw away the last half century
as if your death could be a deal you cut

with genius, in return for fame
and those ferocious poems, blossoming
in the unnatural freeze of '63.
Was it your legend that demanded blood
to prove the violence packed in every lyric

was no pretence? Sadly, it was authentic.
You could have had the man back in your bed
if you'd been willing to endure suspicion. Was hatred
cleaner, did you prefer to damage him
when he saw your healthy body dead?

What if the doctor's number had been used and
you had woken up to Ted's embrace –
seen his remorse – would a new life begin,
would brushing death have kept him safely bound,
was that the happy end you fell asleep in?

Do not rise up now with your red hair
to mock an audience which has come to stare
at the fairground Lady in your story;
explain instead what gamble made you waste
your energy and grace – and the taste of glory.

April Fools' Day

i.m. Isaac Rosenberg (1890–1918)

Does anybody know what it was all for?
Not Private Rosenberg, short as John Keats.
A nudge from Ezra Pound sent him to war,
to sleep on boards, in France, with rotting feet,
writing his poetry by candle ends.
His fellow soldiers always found him odd.
Outsiders do not easily make friends,
if they are awkward – with a foreign God.

He should have stayed in Cape Town with his sister.
Did he miss Marsh's breakfasts at Gray's Inn,
or Café Royal? He longed for the centre
though he was always shy with Oxbridge toffs –
he lacked the sexy eyes of Mark Gertler –
and his *Litvak* underlip could put them off.
'*From Stepney East!*' as Pound wrote
Harriet Monroe, while sending poems to her.

He died on April Fools' Day on patrol
beyond the corpses lying in the mud,
carrying up the line a barbed wire roll
– useless against gunfire – with the blood
and flesh of Death in the spring air.
His was the life half used, if even that,
and the remains of it were never found. We remember:
the iron honey gold, his cosmopolitan rat.

Life Class: A Sketch

In Paris, perhaps. On wet cobbles,
walking alone at night, fragile
and wispily dressed, Jean Rhys,
without a *sou*, past streets
of lit cafés to a meeting place.

Cold to the bone, she has it all planned:
when they go home, she'll fall
at his knees, gaze up like a child,
and make him understand
he cannot abandon her,

lost in a strange land.
His grey eyes are indifferent as
the North Sea to her need –
if she tries to plead her words will drown.

So she smiles instead.
That's how she'll cope with crooks
and pick-ups, drink and veronal
in those grim boarding houses
that now stretch ahead.

Over and over she will write the story
of frail girls and the unkindness of men,
speaking in the voice of her cool notebooks,
until one day a frightened Creole self
climbs down from the attic of memory

in the shape of the first Mrs Rochester,
betrayed, barefoot, imprisoned
in an England of snow and roses,
constrained in Thornfield Hall, a dangerous
ghost – that apparition brings success.

Jean entertains in a Knightsbridge hotel,
elegant in her seventies to meet her fame,
with eyes like dark blue pools:
'Too late,' she says, 'Too late,' without irony,
as her looks fade – into a ninth decade.

Marina's Ghost Visits Akhmatova

> *Our shadows live for ever*
>   – Anna Akhmatova

As Anna dreams, her profile sharp
       as if struck on a coin, Marina is
trudging through frozen mud,
       to the plank over a slope,
a village hut, the nail, a hank of rope…

Anna wakes, her heartbeat uneven,
       warm air against her skin,
in Tashkent where carnations smell of Asia,
       far south from her own
city of water and starvation.

She feels for an old gown – Chinese silk
       embroidered with a dragon,
the seam torn but no matter – trying to think
       only of the world around her:
vodka, peaches, handsome Polish officers,

but she cannot shrug off the shadow
       or her knowledge of
a great poet's death alone.
       She looks over the edge
into the blackness of her own departure,

never guessing she will survive
        another generation of murders,
be surprised by late honours
        and that her last hospital bed
is distant by a quarter century.

Death and the Lemon Tree

I

My foolish indoor tree, this sudden exuberance
        of sweet-smelling flowers troubles me.
Surely it is reckless, when your leaves have been falling
        ever since you were put in the new pot?
Somewhere in your helical code the instructions
        have been fucked up.

Last year I picked your fruit with reverence,
        taking pride in the full flesh.
Today as I feed your roots the intense
        blue crystals for citrus fruit
your heady perfume is no longer rich
        as the low notes of a flute.

Bare wood. Scuffed petals. No question,
        you are under stress.
How can I heal you? More water? Less?
        This is a peculiar season.
I don't even know if it is snow outside the glass

or white blossom torn from the late cherry.
        No matter, for a grey-eyed friend
has taken garden shears to my sick tree,
        and boldly snipped the boughs
saying, 'the roots will search under the soil and spread'.
        Unless, I thought, they are dead.

2

Tinsel hopes. Cold dreams. A year
of ghosts, and the drift of gravel,

away from the shore, the tide between my toes
and no hold against the pull of the sea.

Too many friends are gone, from every
page of my life, and there is even

something treacherous in me, almost
consenting to the whisper of a gentle voice

saying – *weaker by the day, but not in pain,*
and reconciled to dying – sooner rather than later –

Those last words undermine me:
not as a temptation, more

a sudden snuffing out of urgency,
for where is the sense of all this focus

in a rainy June of late-night radio
and mornings spent looking through glass

at a garden of overgrown bushes
and grass too wet to mow. Downhill –

so why not simply coast? It's not my way.
Work is my game. It's how I play.

3

And I shall keep my date to read in Greece –
    Athens in crisis, riots in the Plaka,
but also sunshine, poetry, Mount Parnassus,
    ancient names beckon.

Although in Delphi there is no oracle,
    no cave of murmurs,
in the ruins of Apollo's temple,
    behind broken columns

too heavy for looters, I can hear
    the tread of a history
old as Jerusalem
    and still numinous.

The god himself has vanished
    as if no one ever brought
goats and treasure into his sanctuary
    to beg his healing power.

What the looters missed the Church destroyed.
    Only black basalt of the mountainside
reminds us of Zeus and earthquake,
    stories of a people

old as my own, both seductive
    and a danger to each other.
Their troubles. Our troubles.
    Equally brutal.

On the way back to Athens:
    hillsides of lemon trees
Persian traders brought here from Asia
    along the Silk Road.

They flourish in terraces,
    their progeny immortal
even when neglected,
    surviving centuries.

4

Home again, and what's this? Three or four delicate tips
with a pinky sheen have broken
the grey skin of the lemon branches.
Can these be new leaves?
I am not imagining them. There has been
a vegetable resurrection
in my absence. So, you're not finished yet,
my resilient tree. Good. Let us age further.

Acknowledgements

Some of the New Poems in this volume were first published in *The Spectator*, *Wild Court*, *PN Review*, *Poem*, *Ploughshares*, *Acumen*, and *On Shakespeare's Sonnets: A Poets' Celebration*, ed. Hannah Crawforth and Elizabeth Scott-Baumann (Bloomsbury, 2016).

Index of Titles and First Lines

Poem titles are displayed in *italic*.

Writing to Jane Eyre   18